Beginner's Guide to
Do-It-Yourself

Beginner's Guide to Do-It-Yourself

Tony Wilkins and Ron Grace

PELHAM BOOKS

First published in Great Britain by
PELHAM BOOKS LTD
52 Bedford Square
London WCIB 3EF
1974

© 1974 by Tony Wilkins and Ron Grace

All Rights Reserved. No part of this publication
may be reproduced, stored in a retrieval system,
or transmitted, in any form or by any means,
electronic, mechanical, photocopying, recording
or otherwise, without the prior permission of the
Copyright owner

ISBN 0 7207 0657 2

Set and printed in Great Britain by
Tonbridge Printers Ltd, Peach Hall Works, Tonbridge, Kent
in Baskerville eleven on twelve point on paper
supplied by P. F. Bingham Ltd, and bound by
Dorstel Press, Harlow

Contents

1. Around the House — 9
   Fences; Fence repairs; Gates; Exterior timber; Outside workshop; Paths and paving; Repairs to paths; Garden walls

2. The Exterior of the House — 32
   Painting; Walls; New gutters; Pointing; Outdoor fixing to masonry; Ladder safety

3. Materials, Tools and Security — 45
   Plasterboard; Hardboard; Using laminates; Veneered chipboard; Standard joinery; Glass and glazing; Lubrication; Aerosols and pad brushes; Adhesives; Tools for D.I.Y.; Tool hire; Security

4. Repairs and Jobs Inside the House — 70
   Wall tiles; Dealing with old or damaged ceilings; Cove cornice; Finishing whitewood; Cleaning old furniture; Simple shelving; Jointing methods; Timber trouble; Timber floors; Floor tiles; Parquet flooring; Solid floors; Gaps and cracks; Stairs and repairs; Stair carpets; Curtain rails; Plugging and fixing things to walls; Making a hatchway; Flue troubles; Blocking off a fireplace; Dividing a room; Up aloft

5. Decorating — 106
   Painting tips; Removing a picture rail; Preparation; Painting woodwork; Wallpaper hanging; Hiding humps and bumps

6. Damp and its Cure — 116
   Condensation; Structural damp; Damp floors

7. Noise, Draughts, Ventilation and Cold 123
   Noise; Double glazing; Cavity insulation; Draughts; Freeze-up

8. Plumbing 136
   Central heating; Plumbing system; Copper pipework; Plastics in plumbing; Taps and washers; Ball valves; Tank in the loft; Plumbing tips

9. Electrics 149
   For red, read brown; Ring circuits; Fuses; Wire that plug!

   Index 157

List of Drawings

Repairing a timber fence post	11
Repair bracket for decayed arris rail	12
Repairing a gate	14
Fixing felt to shed roof	19
Insulating and lining a shed	20
Laying a concrete path	23
Three ways of laying paving slabs	26
Bricklaying	29
Brick bonds	30
Fixing gutters	36
Pointing brickwork	38
Wall fixing devices	41
Ladders – safety and security	43
Cutting plastic laminate	49
Tapping glazing sprigs into place	56
Paint pads	59
D.I.Y. equipment that can be hired	64, 65
A selection of security devices	66, 67
Simple circuit for a burglar alarm	69
Tiling a room	85
Cutting a tile to fit	86
Lifting floorboards	90
Curing squeaks in stair treads	94
Removing a picture rail	107
Wall covering	111

Trimming around light switches	112
Ten danger points for damp	119
How sound travels	124
Preventing draughts through overflow	129
Insulating a loft floor	131
Keeping pipework warm	134
Basic plumbing systems	138, 139
Wiring and switching circuits	150, 151
A typical ring circuit	153
Fuse wire and fuses	154

CHAPTER ONE
Around the House

FENCES

A fence can perform a number of different functions. It can keep next door's cat off your flower beds; afford you a degree of privacy; act as a background to a herbaceous border or merely indicate where your garden starts and your neighbour's ends. Price can dictate the type you have, and about the cheapest you can get is chain link fencing. To look its best, it needs straining tightly between posts and, for longest life, it is best to get either plastic-coated fencing or the solid plastic type.

Trellis is reasonably priced, too, but it needs good support. Plastic has come into its own here for you can now get all-plastic trellis which will give years of wear, and stay good looking as well.

Cleft chestnut fencing has always been popular where low price is an important factor, and as the chestnut pales are supported by wire, it is again important that the wire is pulled as taut as possible between posts. An advantage of this type of fencing often overlooked is that it allows daylight and sunlight through to garden plants – an important factor where gardens are on the sheltered side anyway.

Post and rail fencing comes next in price range, and you can govern the cost of your fence merely by slight adjustments to the spacing of the palings. For a really durable type, the all-plastic version has both posts and rails of hollow-section plastic. The cost is higher, but you will never have to paint it.

Where some form of decorative division is needed, posts with plastic chain hung between looks most attractive. The links are tremendously strong as the ingenious process by which the chain is made moulds them without joins.

If more privacy is required, woven panels are economical as

considerable strength can be achieved by weaving together thin sections of timber. Where absolute privacy is wanted, you can buy a special interlocking weave type which really is peep proof. One essential with a more solid fencing is that supporting posts should be very well anchored. Wind pressure can be considerable.

You can add height to a woven fence, or provide something for climbing plants to get a grip on, by adding a foot or two of trellis to the top. Many designs are available which incorporate trellis in the panel.

For maximum security, such as for a boundary fence which you don't want climbed, there is the close board fence. The posts have to be heavy, and boards of considerable section – plus an overlap – so the cost is considerable. It is never wise to skimp on materials, for the effect of wind and sun on poor materials will soon cause warping and the formation of ugly gaps, and the same applies to the cross rails, or arris rails as they are called. These have to carry a lot of weight, so they, too, should be of adequate section, and the posts should not be too far apart, or again you will encourage sagging.

You can buy your fencing materials from your local timber yard and work out for yourself just what you need, or you can take advantage of the number of firms who now supply a variety of fence types in kit form. This is the favourite method, for the company concerned calculates just what you need, and everything comes drilled and cut to length, saving a considerable amount of time and effort.

Do ensure that you choose a reputable firm which has been around for some time. We have encountered one or two firms supplying woven panels which, when made up, are very inferior both in appearance and durability.

A question often asked is which side should the posts be visible when a fence is erected? It is often assumed that you must have the posts your side, but there is no law about this – it is usually just a matter of courtesy. You can have the best face your side, but if you do this, you must ensure that the posts are erected on your land and not on your neighbour's.

FENCE REPAIRS

Maybe you don't want a new fence but just need to do a spot

of maintenance. You will find that the posts are the weak spot of a fence, as they are in direct contact with the ground. If you have loose posts, examine them for damage by rot below ground

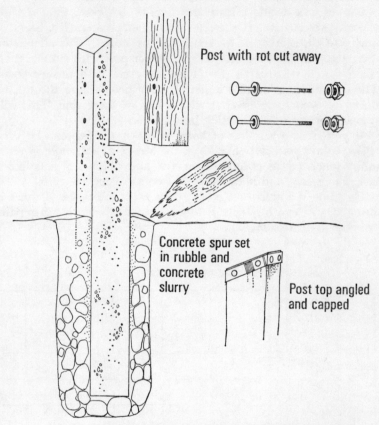

Repairing a timber fence post with a concrete spur

level. An ideal way of dealing with such damage is to use a concrete spur – which you can buy at most builders' yards and many timber yards. Dig a hole for the spur close against the post. Make it at least 2 ft. deep. Cut off the existing post so that its base will rest on the ledge of the spur, and pull out and burn the damaged piece of post.

Pack around the spur with broken brick and stone, ramming

them well down. Then make up a watery mix of concrete and pour it around the spur. The rubble will set as a solid mass. Then you can position the timber post on the spur, bore holes to match those in the spur, and bolt the post in place.

Should you decide to put in a new timber post, treat it with a good preservative. If possible, soak it in preservative. Stand a new post on a layer of broken brick, or stones. This allows for drainage. Fill the hole around the timber post with rubble, then tamp firmly with earth. Don't use concrete with timber posts. Then, to further protect a new timber post, shape the top to throw off water, or cover it with a cap of sheet zinc. This will prevent moisture from getting into the end grain.

If you have a number of holes to make, the job can be very tedious, but you can save time by hiring a post hole borer — many fence suppliers have them available. This tool acts like a large auger bit, and it can save you hours of hard digging.

Examine the arris rails where they enter the posts. If there is damage, you can buy special angle brackets for arris rail repair, or you can make some yourself.

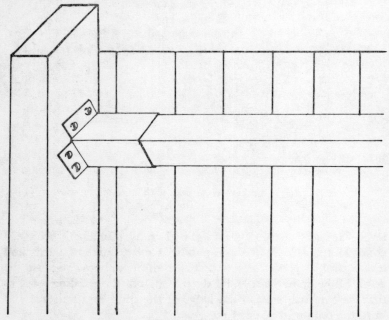

How a decayed arris rail can be supported with a repair bracket

Loose boards should be nailed back as soon as possible. Use galvanized nails or, better still, the excellent aluminium alloy nails which never rust. Drying out and warping of the boards is a common cause of nail loosening, so keep the boards well soaked in preservative, and repeat the process as soon as the boards begin to look dry.

At the base of a close-board fence you should find what is called a gravel board. This takes the brunt of dirty weather, splashed water and heaped earth. As soon as this board shows signs of damage, remove it and replace it with one well soaked in preservative. Again, fix with aluminium nails.

In some exposed situations, you may find a close-board fence is presenting too solid and large a surface to strong winds. The wind pressure can be tremendous. If this is so, you will do well to replace exposed areas with a paling fence or a similar type which allows air to pass through. If you must have close board fencing in such situations, it will pay you to put in concrete posts, well concreted in.

Keep your timber fences well treated with preservative. A good creosote is perfectly adequate except where plants are likely to come into contact with it. The creosote will damage growth. There are special preservatives for use in close proximity to plants.

GATES

Probably the most abused item of garden furniture is the poor old garden gate. It is kicked, slammed and often swung on; if you make a study of gates in your locality you will be amazed how many have given up the struggle! Many householders just give up too, and just have a gap where the gate used to be. But for many of us, with small children or animals, a gate is essential for safety.

One of the main troubles with timber gates is sagging. It may be that the wood has shrunk and joints have loosened. Remove the gate, knock apart the pieces, and re-glue using a waterproof adhesive. At the same time, check for squareness by measuring the diagonals; they must be equal. The brace on a gate is all-important, so make sure it is doing its job by taking the strain. You may need also to cut a piece off a stile (an upright) which is too close to the ground. To lift the gate farther, it is often possible to slip one or two extra washers on the hinge pins.

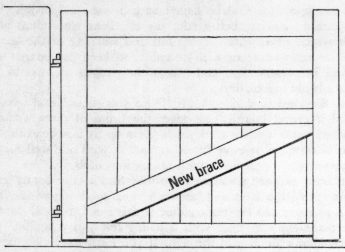

A new brace on a gate will help to stop sagging

Look, at regular intervals, at the state of the paintwork on the gate. Timber is pretty stable all the time it is protected by unbroken paint, but if damp is allowed in the wood will swell, and the paint coating will be pushed off. Chip away all flaking paint with a scraper until you get to sound paintwork. Then prime the bare patches with wood primer, and follow with undercoat and a couple of top coats. You may care to top coat the whole gate, in which case be sure to clean it first with a sugar soap solution or a paint cleaner. Rub down gloss finishes with a pumice stripping block to remove the glaze. Wipe clean, then paint.

Rotted timber in a gate should be ruthlessly cut out. It is no use trying to fill gaps with filler or stopping. It is a waste of time and money. New timber will have to be let-in, then primed and painted as for new work. For even greater protection, use a timber preservative under the primer. With metal gates, keep an eye open for rust. Treat as early as possible by removing loose rust then applying a rust inhibitor, followed by new paint.

If you have to buy a new gate, you will find the rule 'you get what you pay for' applies. Timber or metal gates of very light section or thin gauge are a poor investment. So, if you can, pay a reasonable price. Then spend time applying your paint and so build up a good protective coating.

If you choose hardwood gates and you want a natural finish, use a clear, good quality yacht varnish. Read the instructions on the can very carefully, as it is essential to build up a number of coats to get adequate protection. It is also important that you seal end grain and joints so that the weather cannot get behind the varnish. Failure to watch these points will result in disappointment.

Incidentally, if you choose metal gates with decorative scrollwork, you will find the aerosol paints an ideal way of decorating them.

When your gates are once more in good shape, and are hung, be sure to provide some means of fixing them in the open as well as closed position. Gates have a habit of blowing closed at the most inconvenient times – perhaps just as you back the car out!

Finally, do put a number on your gate or post for all to see. It is a British tradition that most houses have no visible number so that visitors on dark nights have the utmost difficulty in finding the right house.

EXTERIOR TIMBER

Timber is an excellent constructional material for outdoor work provided it is taken care of. All timber is prone to attack by wood-rotting fungi and certain insects, and we tend to forget that this is a perfectly natural process. If you take a look around any wood or forest, you will see that this is how nature gets rid of the dead wood – which is, after all, what you are building with!

Let us hope the day is not far off when all timbers are treated against attack. If you wish, you can buy treated timber, but it is not always easily obtained. For the time being, you must often rely on one of the excellent wood preservatives now available.

The time to treat woodwork is before trouble starts. A regular coat of preservative will keep you out of trouble, whereas neglect often means complete replacement of damaged wood.

There are two main types of job; the protection of rough timbers as used on fence posts, fences, sheds and trellis, and the protection of decorative, and usually highly finished, timbers as used for the cladding of many modern homes.

For rough wood there is a wide choice of protective materials, from creosote through to refined and coloured chemicals. If you choose creosote, make sure it is a good one of well-known name. Some less reputable suppliers have been known to supply stuff more resembling sump oil! And do bear in mind that creosote burns plant life, so don't spill it. For trellis and fencing near plants, use a special preservative that is harmless to your flowers and grass.

You will find that modern preservatives are available in a good range of colours from practically clear, through to black. It is a good idea to try a little out before you start to see that it has the desired effect.

If you have fence posts to replace, soak them in preservative. A simple trough of polythene sheet will do, or use a section of old gutter with the ends stopped off. One coat with a brush has only a superficial effect. If you can't soak the posts, stand the ends in preservative for as long as you can spare. Be sure to shape the top end of your post to shed water, and it pays to cap the top with something like zinc to keep water out of the end.

If you can avoid setting timber posts in concrete, do so. Very often the concrete holds water in contact with the post base – and if you have ever tried to dig out posts set in a huge lump of concrete, you will know what a job it is. Set the posts in rammed rubble, or, as described earlier, better still put up concrete spurs first then bolt the new posts to these.

Where fence boards overlap, and where rails go into posts, it always pays to treat them with preservative before erection – not after. Incidentally, oak posts will give you far longer life, but they are more expensive.

Trellis and woven fencing should be regularly treated with preservative. Once thin slats get the weather in them they soon twist out of shape. Where boards or slats are loose, use galvanized or aluminium nails. These will not rust away, and they won't stain the wood.

Now a word about more decorative uses. Western red cedar is widely used and it looks very attractive. It needs no normal preservatives, as it has its own protective oils. But unless you treat it, it very soon loses that lovely glow and changes to a rather dull grey. There are special protective materials available which contain stains to hold the natural colour. And you will find that a good quality exterior varnish will help preserve the colour, too. Don't forget the good yacht varnishes available. They really stand up to weathering.

Incidentally, Western red cedar is not a good constructional material, it is too soft. But it is good for cladding. If you have difficulty getting nails to grip, there are serrated nails available which do grip well.

With other timber cladding, there are clear preservatives so that you retain the natural colour of the wood, or there is a good range of coloured preservatives – and the colours are really bright. You can also get good quality exterior varnishes to give the wood a sheen, or you can use one of the polyurethane seals. Paints are, of course, preservatives as well as decorative materials. A good three-coat system – primer, undercoat and top coat – will give good protection.

If rot has already taken hold, then treatment is more urgent. Wet rot isn't too bad. This looks like a fine whitish tracery over damp wood, with a musty smell. Although the timber may be very wet, it still has considerable structural strength. If you dry the wood off, the fungus will die.

You often encounter this type of rot on timber door steps, bases of fence posts and on unpainted timber frames. Provided you cure the damp, cut out the damaged wood and inset new pieces, you will get no further trouble.

Dry rot is entirely different. Once it gets a grip, it is very difficult to kill it off. The spores of the fungus are in the air all the time, but they can't multiply on well-ventilated timber with a low moisture content. They like dank, unventilated areas, and once the spores begin to grow, a repulsive fungus is produced, from which large strands spread to surrounding timber and masonry. These strands can carry water to dry timber, wetting it down enough to be attacked – and so the damage spreads. It has been known for dry rot in a basement to end up in the loft, causing serious damage.

The timber is sucked dry of all its cellulose, and the wood becomes brittle, with cracks across the wood grain as well as with it. You can easily put a knife blade into the wood, or your foot may go through it! And you will notice an unpleasant musty smell.

If you find an attack of dry rot, take immediate action. If it is confined to a small area, rip out all affected wood and burn it. Cut well back into sound wood so you are sure you've got out every strand of fungus, then soak the timber in a good wood preservative. If the strands appear on brickwork, before using the preservative, play a blowtorch over the masonry to kill off the spores. But do be careful of fire!

If the rot has a very good hold, passing into masonry, call in a specialist company as soon as possible. True, they charge for their services, but nipping the attack in the bud could be cheaper in the long run. And from the best companies you will get a 20-year guarantee that the area treated will not be attacked again. This can be very useful when selling the property.

Do eliminate likely causes of the trouble. See that all air bricks around the house are clear and add more if necessary. Treat all damp patches as potential trouble. Remember, dry, well ventilated wood is not attacked.

Having dealt with an attack, spend time with shovel, dustpan and brush sweeping up and *burning* all debris. It will contain millions of rot spores just waiting to breed.

OUTSIDE WORKSHOP

An outside workshop is fine in summer, but during winter months it can be a cold, cheerless place where your tools will quickly rust. So a bit of time spent making it weatherproof during the summer months will be well worth while. Have a look, first, at the roof. If it is covered with felt, remember that the stuff doesn't last for ever. Look for cracks and torn areas. Small areas can be patched with a bitumen mastic pressed into pieces of hessian or glass fibre. If you want to do the whole roof, give it a coating of one of the bitumen-latex solutions such as that made by Evode. To add a splash of colour, fine chippings can be added while the bitumen is tacky.

If you decide to cover the roof with new felt, remove all the old material first. Then be sure to unroll the new felt and let it expand a bit before laying it. This will help avoid those ugly bubbles you often see.

The general woodwork of your shed should be protected. If painted, give it a rub down with abrasive paper, seal cracks with exterior grade filler and paint with a good exterior quality paint. If the timber is left in its natural state, a coat of one of the silicone water repellents will help. If the wood has a colour

AROUND THE HOUSE

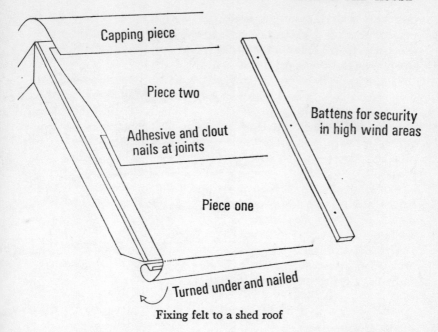

Fixing felt to a shed roof

– such as Western red – choose a preservative with a stain included. This helps keep the rich colour.

It is important that air can circulate under a timber floor, so remove weeds and other greenery from under it, plus any accumulated rubbish. Poor circulation will encourage timber rot. It is not a bad idea to seal off the gap with wire netting so that mice or other animals can't make a home underneath.

Now for the inside. Here, insulation is important. One thickness of cedar boarding offers very poor insulation in really cold weather, even if it does keep the rain out. To improve matters, you can fill the voids between vertical timbers with glass fibre blanket held with drawing pins, then cover the lot with hardboard.

A building paper with a foil face can be used instead of glass fibre; have the foil face into the shed. You can then cover this with plasterboard, insulation board or oil-tempered hardboard. Foil-face building paper on its own is better than nothing. Cover walls, ceiling and floor and you won't get any draughts. Obviously if you use it on a floor you will have to cover the paper with board to protect it.

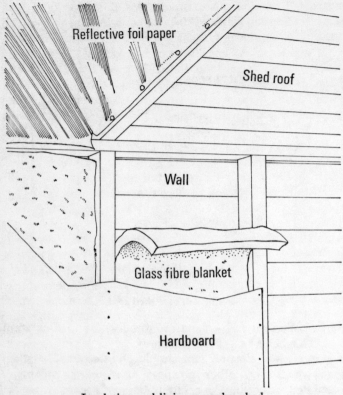

Insulating and lining a garden shed

A useful floor insulation is expanded polystyrene about $\frac{1}{2}$ in. thick with oil-tempered hardboard laid over it. With this you won't suffer with cold feet. Alternatively, use insulation board plus hardboard.

Whatever you choose inside, have a good search for gaps and cracks around doors and windows, and up in the roof or at the eaves. Lumps of mineral wool, glass fibre or odd pieces of polyurethane foam are useful for filling cracks. Don't use newspaper, old socks or materials which encourage insects. For small gaps, use a mastic in strip form, or from a tube.

For heating, it pays to use electricity. It is the safest fuel and can be easily controlled. Use black heat tubular heaters for background warmth and have a switch which incorporates a neon indicator, otherwise it is easy to leave the heaters on when

AROUND THE HOUSE

they are not needed. Fit a fan heater for quick local warmth. Avoid electric fires with red-hot elements. And if you must have a paraffin oil heater, get one that snuffs itself out when knocked over. If condensation is a problem in your shed, remember that for every gallon of paraffin burnt, at least a gallon of water is released. If this settles on your valuable tools, rust can ruin them. Anyway, keep tools greased or oiled, and keep valuable ones in drawers or boxes with a rust-inhibiting paper.

PATHS AND PAVING

There are two ways of tackling paths: by using concrete – either to lay a strip or to form your own blocks – or by buying precast slabs and laying them on prepared ground. The first method offers the most economical way of paving, but not necessarily the most attractive.

If you choose to use concrete, you can, if the areas are large, make use of a ready-mix company who supply by special lorry; an average load is about 3 cu. yd. But you must have easy access to site, or have some willing friends in to help you wheel the stuff round to where it is to be used. Remember, once the lorry arrives, you will have only about an hour in which to place the concrete. Companies offering this service are in the telephone directory yellow pages.

If you prefer to mix your own, as and when required, you can usually get the sand or ballast bagged for a small extra charge. This simplifies storage if space is limited. And you can, for a reasonable fee, hire a concrete mixer which will take all the hard work out of the job.

The first essential with a path is to set out the sides by means of string lines, then clear top soil down to below the proposed concrete thickness – and that means at least 3 in. Use a level and wood pegs to get a true level, levelling from peg to peg. Fill any soft areas with rubble, ramming it well into the ground.

Now you need strong pieces of wood with one dimension equal to the proposed depth of concrete, and these are laid along the sides of the path. Secure the pieces with wood pegs driven into the ground to the outside of the wood lengths, and lightly nail the lengths to these pegs. You can give extra support by knocking a few pieces of brick tight against the inner face of the wood lengths and below the wood surface so that concrete will hide the pieces.

Every 8 ft. or so, fix a piece of wood across the path to divide it into bays. The idea is that you fill alternate bays, ending up with a jointed path. The joints take any slight movement and thus prevent cracking.

If your path adjoins the house, you need a slight 'fall' away from the house – say 1 in. in 6 ft. This will ensure that water does not gather against the house. With any other path, a convex surface helps so that water is shed. A length of timber with a concave surface on one edge will do. This is used for levelling the top surface, moving it along in see-saw fashion.

Now for the mix. The best to use is 1 part fresh cement, 2 sharp sand and 3 parts coarse aggregate by volume – and that merely means by the bucketful. Cement does go off, so it is not wise to rely on the odd bag stored in the garage over the winter months.

To give an idea of amounts needed, 1 bag of cement, $2\frac{1}{2}$ cu. ft. of sand and $3\frac{3}{4}$ cu. ft. of aggregate will produce about $5\frac{1}{2}$ cu. ft. of concrete. It is interesting to note that the total volume of ingredients is quite a bit less than the sum total of the separate ingredients, so this must be kept in mind.

So, a path 90 ft. long and 3 ft. wide by 3 in. thick involves $67\frac{1}{2}$ cu. ft. From this you can calculate just how much of each material you need – based on the amounts given above.

Use the minimum of water for mixing – the less water the stronger the finished concrete. And get the whole mix of even colour. Fill alternate bays just over-full, then use your board to bring the path to shape, see-sawing it across the mix and tamping down any hollows.

When the mix has almost set, a light brush over with a stiff broom will expose the aggregate, making the path non-slip. Never trowel a path. This will make it over-smooth and bring a rich cement deposit to the surface which may later flake away.

When the first alternate bays are set, remove the separating boards and fill the remaining bays, shaping and brushing over, as before. Some folk leave the wood in, but it does tend to rot away after a while, leaving an ugly gap.

Be sure to clean all utensils before the concrete sets on them. If it does persist on certain items, get some Disclean from a builders' merchant and use this to dissolve the deposit. Read the instructions very carefully before using.

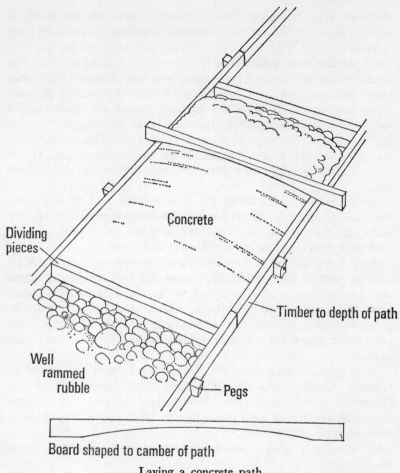

Laying a concrete path

You can make your own slabs for economy using either ordinary grey Portland cement, or adding dry colours to the mix. The more subtle the tone the better. Bright colours can look completely out of place.

The best mix to use for this job is 1 part fresh cement to 3 parts sharp sand by volume. The mix should be a very dry one as this makes it easy to handle and form, and ensures that the concrete is strong. Clear an area of ground and get it dead flat, then surround it with a simple timber frame with the depth of timber equal to the required depth of paving. Make it at least 2 in. thick.

Cover the base within the frame with a bed of sand so the concrete doesn't come into contact with the ground. Now mix your concrete and tip it into the mould. Compact it to remove voids and level off with a length of board see-sawed across the top. Give the concrete half an hour or an hour to begin setting – according to weather conditions. The warmer the day the quicker it will go off. Then use a straight-edge and trowel, cutting right through the concrete with the trowel tip.

Now carefully ease away the timber sections, and leave the concrete to harden. After three or four days, carefully lift the slabs and store them. Leave for two or three weeks before using, and even then don't be too rough with them.

While you are at it, you can produce crazy paving slabs by cutting random shapes with the trowel, not cutting right through the mix this time. Allow a day to set, then break the pieces and leave them to set hard. They look more realistic if you make rectangular slabs then crack them up, but you can't always guarantee getting pieces of the size you require.

The Cement and Concrete Association's book, *Concrete in Garden Making*, available free from the Association at 52 Grosvenor Gardens, London, S.W.1, is a very useful publication, well illustrated with photographs. In it you will find every kind of mix, details of how to lay concrete, how to cast slabs, making crazy paving – plus an excellent section on walls, steps and terraces.

Now what about buying precast materials? The cheapest is to buy broken paving through your local council, and you just take it as it comes. It is not particularly interesting as a material, but it makes reasonable crazy paving. By far the most attractive paving is made from precast slabs of varying sizes and tints, or one of the stone effect slab materials. The best companies supply a chart showing pattern variations, and by marking the area you have to deal with on the chart, you can calculate just what you need of each size.

Now a word of advice based on personal experience. Slabs 2 ft. by 2 ft. are heavy. They can weigh up to 80 lb. each, and if they are stacked at your front gate, you will have a fair job handling them. A wheelbarrow isn't much help. You need a porter's steel trolley.

When laying, you have a choice of three methods. First, you can lay the slabs on a 1 in. bed of mortar. Second, you can use blobs of mortar – one at each corner and one in the middle, or third, you can bed the slabs on a layer of sand. If you use the last method, there is a chance of sinkage or slight rocking. The fun starts when you want to cut slabs – especially if you have to cut to a straight line. You need a wide steel chisel, called a bolster, and a club hammer. Then you need a bed of soft sand on which to lay the slab. It is essential that the slab be dead flat. If there is a high spot somewhere underneath, this will certainly influence the breaking point. Mark the point of cut, then tap gently but firmly along the line until the bolster cuts a vee in the slab. Now if you don't mind a roughish edge, gradually increase the weight of blow until you hear a change of 'ring', and your slab will fracture. Don't be too put out if the cut is at right angles to the one you planned! Put it down to inexperience and try again.

If you want a clean cut, having made one vee, turn the slab over and make an identical score on the other side, gradually increasing weight of blow. The slab should split clean along the marks.

You will find council broken paving hard to cut, for the slabs are very dense. But even so, with a bit of care you can get good results.

The easiest stones to cut are some of the pastel slabs where the mixes are far from dense. Here you must take care not to be too hasty, or your slab will go in all directions before you have really started.

Finally, there is the pointing between slabs. You can use sand, but while it is quick, it soon goes grubby and encourages weed growth. But it does allow water to get away. The more permanent finish is to use a very dry mortar mix brushed into the cracks and pressed home. Again, if drainage is a problem, drill drainage holes at regular intervals.

REPAIRS TO PATHS

New concrete paths and drives can look attractive, but what about those that are getting old? Ground subsidence can cause

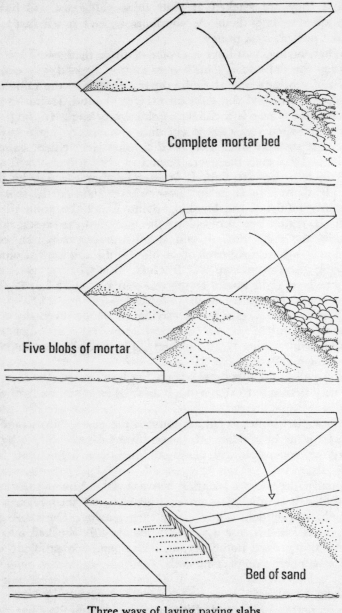

Three ways of laying paving slabs

cracks, frost can flake away the surface. It is then that the surrounds to your otherwise well-kept home can start to look a mess.

One excellent modern way of dealing with this trouble is to use one of the cold asphalt compounds designed for do-it-yourself use to provide an entirely new surface. In the main the compounds are black with specks of white showing, but a rich, warm brown is also available. Apart from the repair jobs they do, the colour can transform the appearance of a house – especially if the walls are of a light colour, when the dark macadam surface will contrast well.

The cold asphalt is supplied in strong paper sacks of about 50 lb. or 100 lb. capacity. If this is your first attempt, order the smaller size because it is easier to handle. With each sack comes a small bag of decorative chippings – but more about those later. A small bag will cover, on average, 20 sq. ft. spread to an initial thickness of $\frac{3}{4}$ in. This varies slightly between manufacturers.

Now let's assume you intend to cover a path. The only tools needed are a garden roller, a rake, a watering can and a tamper for firming down any soft patches of path. The area to be covered must be well consolidated and able to support whatever weight will have to be carried by the path. It is no use spreading cold asphalt over earth, for the asphalt has no load-bearing strength of its own.

Next, if there are weeds and grass growing through the old concrete, treat the path with a killer that is not creosote based. Although the new macadam will discourage growth it may not stop it, so the killer will ensure no future trouble. The next job is to give the path a thorough sweep to remove all loose materials. Potholes and gaps must be filled with firmly packed rubble or concrete, and this is the time to ensure that the path is cambered or sloped to shed rainwater, and that no areas will encourage puddles. You can fill large potholes with the compound, but it can work out a rather expensive way of preparing the path.

Some firms supply a priming emulsion to brush on to the path before the asphalt is laid. Others say no primer is needed, and this is something to check on when you buy. Take your first bag of asphalt, tip it in the middle of the area to be covered, then rake out out to a thickness of $\frac{3}{4}$ in. Give the garden roller a really good wetting with water to prevent the asphalt from sticking to it, then roll.

Before the surface is too well compact, you can add a sprinkling of the chippings which will further enhance the appearance. Take a tip, and use them sparingly. Usually there are more than you need, and if you overdo it your path will look as if it is time the snow was swept from it! A final rolling will consolidate the chippings.

Carry on, bag by bag, until the whole path is finished. Then the path can be used immediately. Although the surface is hard, it will continue to harden for about another week – so don't be too rough with it initially. The flux oils used to keep it soft and workable in the bag gradually evaporate, and you are left with a really tough, new surface. But even if you should damage the surface, an area can easily be cut out and a patch inserted, which will very quickly blend in. This sequence suggested for a path can just as effectively be applied to your drive, and the surface will take the weight of a car immediately after rolling.

GARDEN WALLS

Small garden walls can enhance a garden considerably and apart from appearance, they hold back soil banks and flower borders, make weeding easier, and they keep grass at bay.

Probably the cheapest walling material is to make your own briquettes from concrete. These are made in the same way as paving slabs, described earlier. To lay the briquettes, you need to clear the top soil for a depth of at least 4 in., and make your foundation area at least 4 in. wider than the wall width. Use pegs, string and a straight-edge to get your foundation dead level, then lay your foundation using a 1 cement, $2\frac{1}{2}$ sand 4 coarse aggregate mix. This should be about 3 in. thick, and it should be level lengthwise and across the width.

Damp the bricks before using them to prevent suction, then lay them using a mortar composed of 1 part cement to 3 parts soft sand. Add a little P.V.A. liquid as a plasticiser and binder. You can point your wall with the same mix. If you prefer you can get mortar ready-mixed in a paper sack. You add only water, and it gives a nice buttery mix. Don't add too much water or the mortar will run.

If you think making your own briquettes is too much of a

AROUND THE HOUSE

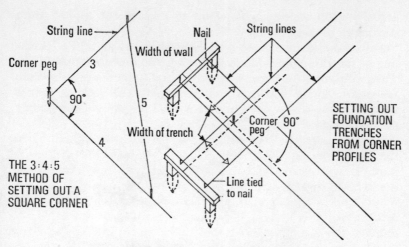

Bricklaying – setting out a corner

fag, you can make very presentable walls using broken paving or flags. As with path making, the paving will have to be cut to size. Wear gardening gloves, or you will cut your hands to pieces.

Next up in price are the very attractive walling materials produced by such people as Redland, Marley, Kentstone and Noelite. They come in a wide range of pastel colours, and very attractive they look too. All the firms we know offer leaflets, so there is no need to give more details on this score. You can of course use ordinary bricks, new or secondhand, and if you want more information on wall construction, then the Cement and Concrete Association booklet mentioned earlier is very useful.

High walls have certain disadvantages in the average garden. They keep light and air and sun from plants, and they give you a boxed-in feeling. One good method if you want to stick to walling instead of fencing is to use decorative screen blocks. The immediate advantages are: daylight and air gets through, they look very attractive, and they afford privacy without a feeling of being caged in. Standing at right angles to a wall, you can chat to the chap next door, but look at the wall obliquely – as perhaps you would from your lounge – and the wall looks solid.

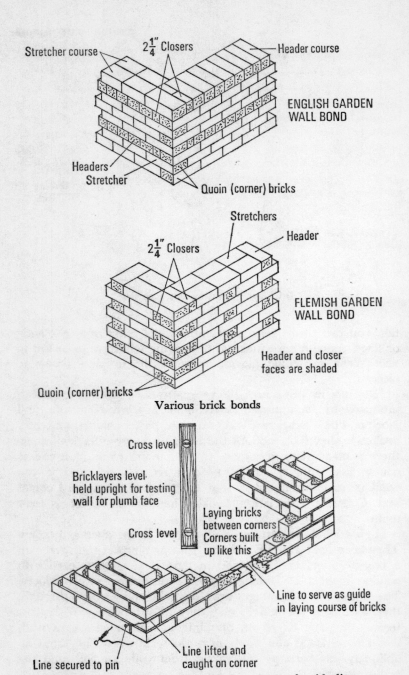

Blocks come in a variety of patterns, and with many of them, by turning them around or using varying combinations, very many patterns can be produced. Laying can be a bit tricky at first, as you have to butter with mortar surfaces which are to be far from horizontal, but you soon get the knack. Again, manufacturers supply excellent literature to help you both with patterns and laying.

One word of caution; don't use too much walling in confined spaces; it gets overpowering. You really need to be able to get away from it to see it at its best.

CHAPTER TWO
The Exterior of the House

PAINTING

Surprisingly few handymen paint the outsides of their homes. True, it is a bind of a job, but it can be an expensive one to have done. If you are willing to tackle bits of it over a planned period, it needn't be too much of a chore.

Here are a few tips that may prove helpful. Even if you don't paint every year, have a washing down session with weak sugar soap to remove grime. This dirt very soon eats into the paintwork, breaking it down to let the weather in, so even washing down will make the paint last longer. If paint is merely grubby when you want to repaint, don't strip it off unless you really must. Use a good paint cleaner to remove dirt, then rub over with a pumice stripper block, keeping the pumice damp but not too wet. This will take the gloss off the paint and remove any nibs (uneven spots due to dirt or bubbles), preparing it for repainting.

Wash down with clean water and allow to dry. If you are changing colour, follow with undercoat, then two top coats. Where paint has broken down in only a few places, again it is as well not to strip the lot. Rub down the flaking areas until you are sure the rest is sound, then touch in the areas with undercoat to bring them flush with the rest of the paintwork. Then you can paint over the lot. If you should go through to bare wood when rubbing down, the bare areas must be primed before further paint is applied.

If the paintwork is badly damaged, then the lot should be stripped off. A blowlamp is certainly the cheapest way of tackling the job, but take care around windows and near the eaves. You can easily crack glass in windows, and set fire to old nests in the eaves. The safer, but more expensive, method is to

THE EXTERIOR OF THE HOUSE

use a chemical stripper. Let the paint wrinkle well before you strip it off. And you may well need two coats of stripper.

When all the paint has been scraped off, be sure to neutralise the chemical as advised on the container. If there is any crack or gap filling to do, use cellulose filler prior to priming, but putty after priming. The reason is that putty must not be allowed to come into contact with bare wood as the oil in the putty will soak into the wood, weakening the putty. So you prime first, preventing oil from reaching wood. If you use cellulose filler, be sure to choose exterior grade. Knots in wood can be a problem, too, as resin can bleed from them. If you encounter any, seal them with patent knotting prior to priming.

Metalwork needs especial care wherever rust is encountered, for rust can spread under a paint film, gradually pushing it off. If you encounter rust, strip back the paint until no further rust can be found, then treat the bare area with a good rust inhibitor. Once this is dry you can repaint. Large areas of rust should be wire-brushed – and if you do this job be sure to wear protective glasses of some kind. They could save you from a nasty accident.

If, when painting, you find gaps between frames and brick-work – perhaps due to shrinkage of timber, be sure to seal the gaps. The best material for this job is a mastic filler injected into the gap and smoothed over. This will surface-harden, but the material will retain its adhesion and flexibility. Putty or cement, on the other hand, can soon crack away and fall out should there be any further movement or shrinkage.

If you do tackle your exterior decorating over a period of time, do plan work so that wood or metal is never left bare. Get a coat of protection on before leaving off work for the day.

WALLS

When considering the brickwork, the first job is to decide whether it should be painted anyway. If your home has pleasant facing bricks which look a little jaded, leave them well alone – or at most give them a good rub over with half a brick of the same type. Painted brickwork can look terrible and, once done, there is little chance of going back. You can further smarten such walls by repointing perhaps with a lighter colour mortar to give contrast (more about this later) but it is not advisable to paint existing mortar a lighter colour. The result can look very artificial and cheap.

If brickwork is poor, it may be worth considering a rendering over the lot, though this is quite a big task. The Cement and Concrete Association of 52 Grosvenor Gardens, London, S.W.1. can advise you on mixes and on all aspects of concrete use. A smooth finish is hard to achieve. Far better put on a roughcast finish. To do this you can hire what is called a Tyrolean projector, which literally flings a wet cement mix on to a wall with most attractive results. This is easier to do than the old spar and pebble dash which involves a lot of mess and waste in inexperienced hands.

You can slap a wall paint over the bare brickwork, but unless yours is an olde-worlde cottage-type home which would have been whitewashed in the old days, the result will probably look like poor bricks painted!

Assuming you have a rendered wall that wants painting, the first job is to go over the walls with a wire brush to remove all loose and flaking materials. If the wall was whitewashed this must either be washed off, or the wall sealed with a special petrifying liquid so that any new paint has a secure base.

Next rake out any cracks in the rendering, damp them and fill with mortar to which has been added some P.V.A. emulsion. This acts as an adhesive, holding the new material in the cracks.

You have a choice of excellent materials ranging from stone paints and cement paints through to emulsion paint and special plastic coatings. Some paints incorporate special aggregates. These may be fine leaves of mica or nylon fibres – to mention but two – and the aggregate acts as a filler and texturiser, giving a very tough, weather-resistant surface. Whatever you choose, make sure that it is recommended for external use, and make dead sure that the surface to which it is applied is clean and sound.

Calculating how much you need can be a headache, but you should find information on the can. Bear in mind that a real textured finish can need nearly twice as much paint as a smooth rendering, and a new rendering will need more than one already painted.

Now, a word on weatherproofing walls. Of course, all the paints just mentioned will do a good job, and will keep the weather out, but what about plain decorative brick? Here, you can protect effectively with a silicone water repellent or similar material. Most don't radically alter the appearance of the brickwork, though some have a slight tint added just so you can see where you have treated. This disappears after a few hours. We find it is best to flood the material on so that it just starts to flow down the wall. The effect of such a repellent is to prevent water getting into the wall, yet still allow moisture trapped in to evaporate out. In other words, the wall can still breathe.

A note of caution. Make sure your damp proof course is in good shape before you seal the walls. A slight fault may not be apparent due to evaporation of moisture, but when the wall is sealed and evaporation is restricted, damp may try to rise up the walls.

Finally, what do you do if you are just fed up with the general appearance of your walls? Well, why not consider covering an area with cedar shingles, cedar boarding or plastic boarding? You can make it so you won't recognise the old place.

NEW GUTTERS

Gutters take a lot of punishment over the years. Corrosive chemicals in the atmosphere are deposited on the roof by rain, and washed into them; snow and ice weigh them down, and corrosion and rust eat them away where painting has been neglected.

If your gutters are in pretty poor shape, why not take the plunge and fit new ones? The job is nowhere near as difficult as it used to be since the introduction of plastic rainwater goods. To start with, they are only a fraction of the weight of cast iron, so erecting new gutters is possible by one person. But don't take any chances in getting the old stuff down. You need at least two people securely planted on good ladders to get down the heavy old sections.

Plastic gutters have many advantages over old types. They need no painting; the smooth surfaces do not collect dirt; water flows more freely in them and, of course, the plastic will never rot or rust. There has, in the past, been a fair amount of resistance to them, because being much lighter in section, they don't give the appearance of being very robust. In fact the material is very strong and resilient. It may bow under the weight of snow, but when the pressure is eased, it will merely snap back into place again. This was proved in the severe winter of 1963 – the first real test for plastic gutters. To our knowledge there was not a single complaint of failure.

Another common fear is that the gutters will not take the weight of a ladder plus user. They will, quite easily, but there is a danger that should be allowed for. Plastic gutters are extremely smooth, and an unsecured ladder may slide away. So be sure to secure your ladder by means of rope through a ring bolt screwed into the fascia board, which is the wood that the gutter brackets are fixed to. While on the subject of snags, bear in mind that if you clean off paint with a blowlamp and get too near your new gutters, you may very well melt them! Best take them down. It is easy enough.

Systems vary, but generally you have sturdy plastic brackets which are screwed to the fascia board. Don't over-tighten screws. You will find full details in the literature supplied, but be sure to get a steady fall to the down pipes. And take a tip from us, and study a leaflet very carefully against the dimensions of your roof before ordering your materials. It may be you will have to cut lengths of gutter to fit an exact distance. You will also have to allow for getting around corners, and this takes a little more gutter than you would at first imagine.

Gutter lengths clip into the brackets, and usually seat on a

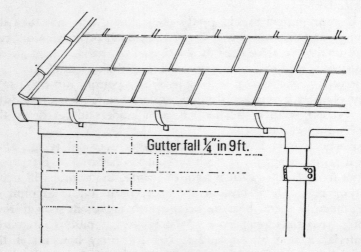

Fixing gutters – getting the correct slope

neoprene gasket which gives a watertight seal. Cutting off a piece, or filing a new slot is extremely easy with hacksaw and file.

Down pipes are even easier to fit. They may be just a push fit, or you may have to apply a little solvent to weld the joint. By the way, while you are at it, fit cages in the tops of down pipes to keep rubbish out and to prevent birds from nesting. Actually, plastic net makes excellent gutter guards, keeping leaves and rubbish out of the gutters too.

What happens if you have a semi, and the chap next door wants to keep his cast iron gutters? Don't despair, you can get a special jointing piece designed to join old ogee pattern to new half round. Also, if you want your garage to match the house, you can get a lighter weight of gutter with which to smarten it up.

POINTING

That mortar joint between your brickwork is important. If crumbly and soft, it may allow rain to get in. If decayed and dirty it can spoil the appearance of a whole wall. Here are a few tips on repairs to pointing and the materials you need.

First you need to rake out all the old mortar to a depth of $\frac{1}{2}$ in. to $\frac{3}{4}$ in. You can do this with a cold chisel, but there are special routing tools available which fit into electric drills and make the job so much easier.

The simplest material to use for repointing is a ready-mix material. You can get this from most large builders merchants and all you need to add is water. Keep your mix as dry as possible so it doesn't dribble down the brickwork. And just before pointing, damp the joints with water applied with an old paintbrush. This stops the porous brickwork sucking all the moisture from the mortar and weakening it.

Apply the mortar with a small pointing trowel bringing the mix just proud of the wall surface. Do the vertical bits first, then the horizontal runs. Keep the mortar off the face of the wall!

The trickiest job comes next. That of getting a neat finish. The simplest way is to produce what is called a hollow joint by rubbing along the joint with a bent piece of $\frac{3}{8}$ in. diameter mild steel rod. A piece of old bucket handle is a good substitute. Alternatively you can produce a flush joint. You need a straight

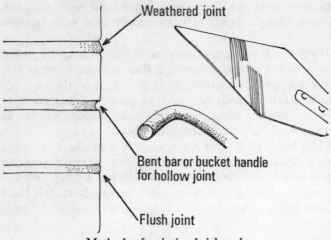

Methods of pointing brickwork

length of wood held just below the joint, then a simple little tool known in the trade as a Frenchman. It is a piece of strip metal bent up at the end to form a cutting edge, and it is the edge drawn along the joint which shaves off the unwanted mortar.

If you feel a bit more ambitious – you need to match surrounding pointing – you can, with practice, produce a weathered joint. This is angled like the slope of a roof, and it deflects water off the course of bricks below. This is one of the hardest of joints to form, but practice with the pointing trowel held at the correct angle will soon give you the idea.

The colour of the pointing can greatly affect the overall appearance of the wall, so if you want something a little more dramatic, why not try coloured mortar? You can buy white cement to which can be added dry colour. You can, of course, use the colours with ordinary Portland cement, but the colours are dulled by the greyness of the cement. Don't go too bright, and do try a small area first and let it dry before you finally decide to do the lot.

The mix to use if you are mixing your own mortar is 1 part cement, 3 parts clean soft sand plus the addition of a proprietary plasticiser. Amounts will be recommended on the packet. Use as little water as possible. It isn't wise to mix more mortar than you can use in about half an hour.

THE EXTERIOR OF THE HOUSE

Should you spill or drip mortar on your brickwork, it can very easily spoil the decorative effect – but don't panic! Don't try to rub it off. Let it set, then get some of the acid cleaner that builders use for cleaning off their tools after doing a concreting job. You should be able to get some from a builders merchant. Apply it just to the split mortar, which it will dissolve without affecting the brickwork.

As a general rule, try to keep mortar off decorative surfaces. Protect paths, porch roofs and tiles with polythene sheet or building paper. It is far easier to keep the mess off than to clean it up afterwards.

OUTDOOR FIXING TO MASONRY

The traditional way of fixing anything to a wall was a hefty great wedge hammered into a mortar joint – but times have changed, though some tradesmen still seem to disagree. There are more sophisticated and more effective ways today, so here are a few of them.

For jobs like fixing trellis, securing plants and anchoring plant wires, the masonry nail or pin is ideal. If you have no experience of them, do make sure that you get the right size, for penetration into actual masonry is very small indeed. If you hammer in too far, you can split a brick quite easily by wedge action.

For rough fixing, cut nails, or flooring nails, can be used provided the mortar in the joints is not too hard. Hammer only into joints, not into brick. Some modern lightweight blocks can be nailed into – or screwed into – but these are not common in exterior construction. For jobs where screws are preferred, asbestos fibre plugging compound does a good job, and the screw can be removed and replaced as required. Holes should not be over-large, but slight irregularity doesn't matter.

A little more refined is the plastic anchor, and a number of types are available. The hole drilled to take it must be the right size, and it is best to buy the type of anchor which has wings to prevent the plug from rotating as the screw is driven home. If you make the hole too big, the whole lot revolves, anyway! Do make sure your hole goes deep enough to take the plug and screw. If you bottom too soon, the whole lot will work loose or get chewed up.

Incidentally, expanding anchors are available with a hook

fitting which is ideal for clothes lines or catenary wires (steel wires to support electrical cables – for example, for a power supply to a garage at the bottom of the garden). You merely push the anchor in, turn the hook, and presto, the job is done.

For really fine fixings where you don't want a large hole, there are Rawlset anchors which take a $\frac{5}{32}$ in. or $\frac{3}{16}$ in. Whitworth screw. The expanding shell section is brass, so it will not rust or corrode.

What about fixing gate posts or timbers to walls for lean-tos and the like? The items so far mentioned are not, in our estimation, designed for this kind of loadbearing. Choose the Rawlbolt, which gives a very secure anchorage with the minimum of trouble. A Stardrill will make the correct size hole – absolutely essential. There are Stardrills to match the Rawlbolt sizes, and they are cross-referenced. Make sure you get the right drill for the right bolt. The drill is used in conjunction with a hammer, and you rotate the drill a fraction after each hit. It is a mistake to use a really heavy hammer. Steady, firm tapping is far superior to heavy blows.

As the actual bolt is turned home into the Rawlbolt shield, a special wedge nut forces four serrated segments apart, and a very firm fixing results. Hook or eye Rawlbolts are available if you need them.

If you have special fixing jobs to do, such as bolting down a shed to a concrete base, or locating a timber home extension on a brick base, there are special Rawlplug fixing devices which can help you. Enquire at your local stockist for details before you start the cement work. It may be that you would do best to use something like cement-in sockets.

So far, we have dealt with hand tools, but you can use a tipped masonry drill in a power tool for hole making, preferably with some form of speed reducer. The average D.I.Y. drill is operating at much too high a speed to get best effect. If you have never drilled masonry, short, sharp bursts of pressure are best. Withdraw the drill regulary to allow it to cool. When it starts to whistle, it's time to get it sharpened!

The last word, as far as hole drilling in masonry is concerned, is the hammer drill. As the chuck rotates, a special mechanism imparts thousands of sharp blows endwise on the masonry bit, giving excellent penetration.

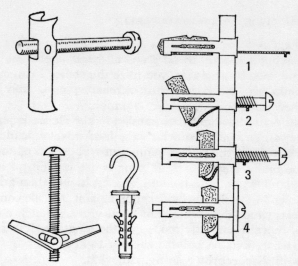

A selection of wall fixing devices. *Top left:* Rawlplug gravity toggle. *Bottom left:* Spring toggle. *Centre:* Fischer wallplug, type SB, fitted with a nylon-coated metal hook. *Right:* Fixing a Viking toggle plug (Bostik). 1. Insert toggle. 2. Push screw in – base of toggle will tilt. 3. Engage screw and pull outwards, to bring base towards hole. Remove screw. 4. Position article to be fixed replace screw, and tighten

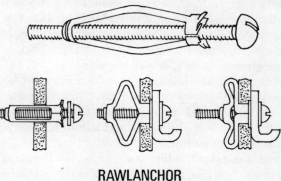

RAWLANCHOR

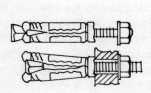

RAWLBOLT

LADDER SAFETY

When buying a ladder, avoid a second-hand one unless it is in good condition. Buying new, you have the choice between wood and aluminium. Wood is perfectly reliable, reasonably cheap, but rather on the heavy side. Aluminium is durable, rather more expensive, but lighter to handle; so the choice is yours.

When you buy, make sure that the ladder will extend at least three rungs above the highest point you will ever need to reach; this is normally gutter level. If your house is built on a slope, bear in mind that one wall could be a lot higher than another.

If you choose a timber ladder, don't paint it. This could hide any defects which develop. Put on clear varnish that you can see through. Store it correctly too, as in the diagram. If it must be stored outside, make a polythene cover to keep the worst of the weather off. For security reasons, padlock it.

Raising an extending ladder over about 10 ft. extension is a two man job. Get a helper to put his foot on the first rung, then you raise the ladder, working along the rungs. Carry the ladder in the vertical position to the job, and erect it so that the base is placed a quarter of the height from the wall. Thus, if the ladder is 12 ft. long, the base should be 3 ft. from the wall. See that the base is on something really firm. If it has to stand on earth, make a simple timber platform. If the base is on smooth concrete, lash the base to something firm, such as a stake in the ground nearby, or a down pipe.

Secure the top of the ladder, too, as slipping must be avoided. This applies particularly if you have plastic gutters which, though very tough and well able to take a ladder, are very slippery. An eye bolt in the fascia and length of rope is one way of doing this, and it's well worth the bother.

Don't use a standard ladder for roof work. If you must work up there, borrow or hire a roof ladder which is made for the job.

When working on your ladder, see that your shoes are free from mud so that your feet cannot slip. Never lean off balance, or reach far to one side, and remember to take all the tools you need to the job. You can get a ladder tray for holding tools, and an S hook on one of the higher rungs is ideal for holding a paint can. But don't reposition a ladder with tools still up on the tray. You may get a shower of tools about your ears!

Another useful aid is a ladder spacer; a device which pulls the top of the ladder away from the wall, and, at the same

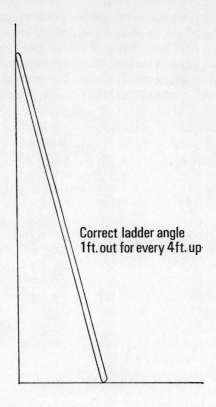

Correct ladder angle
1 ft. out for every 4 ft. up

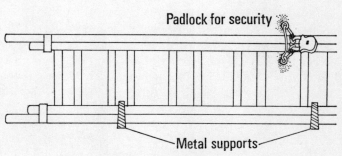

Padlock for security

Metal supports

Ladders – safety and security

time, anchoring it by means of rubber tips on the spacer arms. An ordinary plank can be useful, too, when working at a window. Lashed to the top of the ladder, it can bridge the gap between ladder and frame. If you have walls to paint, get another ladder and a couple of brackets designed to support planks, and build yourself a simple scaffold. Or hire a scaffold kit. A ladder can be a very uncomfortable perch for hours on end.

CHAPTER THREE
Materials, Tools and Security

There is a material which could be made far more use of in the handyman field, and that is gypsum plasterboard. This is a sandwich material consisting of a core of set gypsum plaster faced either side with a sheet of heavy paper. The most common thickness is $\frac{3}{8}$ in. which costs in the region of $2\frac{1}{2}$p a square foot; $\frac{1}{2}$ in. is a bit more expensive. There is also a grade with an aluminium foil backing which gives the board good insulation properties. This costs about 3p for the $\frac{3}{8}$ in. grade.

Plasterboard is the ideal lining material. It is easy to handle and cut; cheap when compared with many boards, and it is naturally fire-resistant. If you have to remove old plaster down to the brick in an older house, use plasterboard to dry line the wall. And for lining the loft or replacing an old ceiling, plasterboard is ideal.

There are two main methods of fixing plasterboard to a wall. When using battens, the wall should be clean and dry, and the battens should be about 2 in. by 1 in., with the 2 in. face to the wall. Nail or screw the battens in place. Then the boards may be used horizontally or vertically, making sure that they overlap the edge batten by only half so there is half left for the adjacent board. Battens should be spaced at 1 ft. 6 in. centres for $\frac{3}{8}$ in. board and 2 ft. for the $\frac{1}{2}$ in. board. Use galvanized plasterboard nails for fixing, and drive them just below the surface of the board but not too hard or you will tear the paper.

Where the wall needs to be decorated, use what are called taper-edge boards. When boards are butted together the tapers meet, forming a hollow over which special jointing tape and joint filler is used to give an invisible joint. There are square edge boards too, and these would be adequate in, say, a loft where appearance doesn't matter.

45

The second method of fixing is by means of plaster dabs, usually known as the dot and dab method. No battens are needed, but small pieces of thin millboard are bedded to the wall with gypsum plaster to give support to board edges, then thicker plaster dabs are applied between them on to which the board is pressed.

Of course if you have a wall of modern lightweight blocks or perhaps of breeze, then you could apply your plasterboard direct to the wall using nails. But bear in mind the wall must be flat if your new wall surface is to be true.

As the wall has been dry lined, the new surface may be painted or papered at once. As the name implies, there is no initial drying out period. If you are interested in any aspect of the use of plasterboard, drop a line to British Gypsum Ltd., D.I.Y. Advisory Service, Ferguson House, 15–17 Marylebone Road, London, N.W.1. You will find them very helpful and they can offer some excellent booklets on the subject.

HARDBOARD

Hardboard is, in the main, a medium or high density material made of wood fibres mashed and compressed. It has the advantage of being grainless. That means it won't split, chip or delaminate in use. And it has a highly finished surface which is easy to decorate.

There are two main types of hardboard. First there is standard hardboard which is suitable for most jobs about the house. It can be worked with all normal woodworking tools, and it can be bought in colours ranging from deep brown through to a light cream.

Then there is oil tempered or super hardboard. This is a tougher board with a much higher resistance to weather. It can in fact be used for exterior jobs, and it is also ideal as a floorcovering which needs only a decorative seal. Standard tools can also be used for oil tempered boards.

There are of course other members of this family, but the difference is one of appearance rather than content. Perforated hardboard – or pegboard as it is probably better known – is available in a variety of hole patterns. In the kitchen, a wall faced with pegboard fittings ranging from shelf bracket to simple hooks. Pegboard is also an ideal facing for a workshop wall if used with metal or plastic spring clips.

Decorated boards are now widely used, from the imitation tile patterns to the plain boards in a variety of colours, plus mosaic patterns. These are usually stove enamelled and will withstand considerable wear, though they are not recommended as working surfaces. Moulded and embossed boards are not seen so often, but are really effective if you want a relief pattern. There are also tiles, reeds, flutes, leather grains, wood grain effects and perforated types.

Now what about working hardboard? Priority number one is conditioning. This entails damping the rough back of the board, then laying it flat – or back to back with other boards – for a period of forty-eight hours, preferably in the room in which the board will be used. In this way, the moisture content of the board is adjusted and there is far less likelihood of buckling.

To cut the board, lay it smooth side up and cut with a medium to fine saw. A sheet saw, which has a blade shaped so that it never binds, is a good alternative, but you can use a normal hand saw as long as the teeth are not too coarse. For really large jobs, a power saw attachment for a power tool is ideal. It takes all the effort out of the work. Edges can quickly be cleaned up with glasspaper, preferably fixed around a block of wood. For smoothing and trimming you can use a shaping tool fitted with a woodcutting blade.

When it comes to fixing, make sure you get the right kind of nails for the job. Special pins are made for hardboard, and our favourites are the rustless, deep-drive panel pins. These have diamond shaped heads, and though they are not so easy to hit square, the heads sink well into the board, leaving only a small hole to be filled.

You can, of course, fix hardboard with any of the contact adhesives available. Apply adhesive to both surfaces, allow to dry and press together for instant stick. A rubber hammer can be used to make sure the bond is good.

If you are fixing your board to a framework, remember that the board should be supported at about 1 ft. 2 in. centres, and of course on all edges. If your spaces are much more than this, you will get sagging, unless you switch from the normal $\frac{1}{8}$ in. board to $\frac{1}{4}$ in. hardboard. If that sounds thick, just think – you can get hardboard $\frac{1}{2}$ in. thick!

As for decorating, most boards need sealing first with a hardboard sealer to prevent suction, but there are now a number of boards which are primed ready for painting. If you can get hold of this type you will find the priming or sealing coat is far smoother than you can get with a brush. After sealing, the choice of paint is entirely up to you. For hardboard flooring all you need is a seal such as Ronseal or Bourne Seal, and you have a really durable and inexpensive floorcovering.

Folk often ask about bending board – say for a pelmet. Standard hardboard can be bent to a fairly tight curve provided that the board is given a really thorough soaking first. Experiment with scrap pieces first, for when a board snaps, it gives no warning.

If you want neat edges to your hardboard, look out for plastic mouldings, either for single edges, or for internal and external corners. They can make all the difference to the finish of a job.

If you would like further information on this versatile material, drop a line to FIDOR (the abbreviated name of the Fibre Building Board Development Organisation Ltd.), at Stafford House, Norfolk Street, London, W.C.2. They have some excellent advisory leaflets, and will be only too pleased to assist you.

USING LAMINATES

Laminated plastic is an ideal material for worktops, and it makes a good cladding for all kinds of furniture. The laminate consists of a base material on which is laid a paper pattern, then the whole sheet is sealed with a layer of melamine. It is therefore important not to cut through the melamine layer, because once the pattern is damaged, there is little you can do in the way of repair work.

You will note that most laminates recommended for working areas have a random pattern which doesn't show scratches. A plain colour may look good, but it can show scratch marks, so keep the plains for vertical and other non-work surfaces.

The best tool for sheet cutting is the Stanley knife fitted with a laminate cutting blade or the Cintride tungsten carbide tipped cutting tool. If you run the blade along a straight-edge making a lot of passes so the blade scratches into the surface, you will cut through to the pattern. Then you can snap the sheet cleanly by lifting the sheet ends up towards you. Never bend the other way or you will have an uneven break.

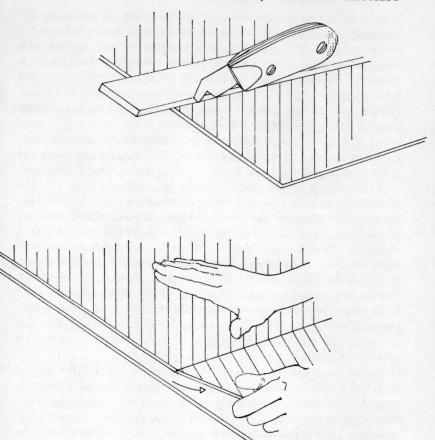

Cutting plastic laminate: scoring and breaking towards the finished surface

Two tools have appeared in recent years and both are selling well. These are the Goscut and the Mole Supercut, designed for cutting shapes in laminates and metal sheets. While they are very useful for shaping work, we do not recommend them for long runs as they are very tiring on the wrist. Another way of tackling long runs if you haven't a knife is to use a sheet saw such as the Aven Varisaw. Latest tool for cutting laminates is the Merlon power-drill attachment. Always work with the pattern up when cutting with a saw. The only exception to this rule is if you use a power saw or the Merlon attachment.

To smooth the edge of your cut laminate, use a rasp or a throwaway blade plane (such as the Stanley) fitted with a laminate cutting blade. Finish off with a cabinet scraper; This gives a really silky finish. If you are covering a surface, such as a table top, allow $\frac{1}{8}$ in. overlap until the sheet has been stuck in place, then trim back neatly.

To cut a circle in laminate you need to make a circular template, anchor it in place with double sided tape, then cut around it with a laminate knife, working slowly and surely until you cut right through. Clean up with glasspaper.

Contact adhesive is now widely known, so here is a tip for positioning a sheet accurately. Use the siliconised backing paper kept from Con-Tact or Fablon. Lay this on the glued surface – it won't stick. You can then lay the laminate on top; move it about until accurately in place, then slide out the paper. You can do a similar job with thin laths, or even brown paper, but the siliconised material slips more easily. When the laminate is in place, tap it home with a rubber mallet. If you haven't got one, use an ordinary hammer and a block of wood. Lay the wood on the laminate, then hit it. Never clout the laminate or you will damage it.

Laminate edges can just be left exposed, or slightly angled with the cabinet scraper. Or you can buy a special plastic or aluminium edging strip designed to hide the laminate edge. These are either pinned or stuck in place, depending upon type. Another neat finish is to glue or pin a strip of hardwood in place, smooth with glasspaper, then finish with a wood seal or varnish.

If you want to be ambitious and cover larger areas, you can buy special plastic channellings into which whole sheets can be slotted. You can get them for internal and external angles too, so whole walls can be covered.

Finally, don't throw away off-cuts of laminates. They make excellent table mats and cutting boards.

VENEERED CHIPBOARD
Veneered chipboard comprises a core of dense, good quality chipboard faced with a decorative veneer. There are a variety of finishes, including mahogany, teak and oak, and there is

MATERIALS, TOOLS AND SECURITY

whitewood for painted work. There are also two main types of veneering available, and it is worth noting the difference. First, there is a straight veneer with an attractive grain pattern, with every board different. Second, there is what can be described as a laminated veneer, where a lot of pieces of veneer are stuck on top of one another to form a very thick sandwich, then a veneer is sliced off the edges. The effect is a very even veneer with no grain pattern. Of course, the advantage here is that every board will look like its neighbour – a valuable asset to the furniture maker.

It is also worth noting that most manufacturers now offer leaflets or booklets with designs, and if you have never worked with these boards, it will pay you to get hold of a few designs and see how the boards are used. The whole secret of design is to plan your units to fit available sizes of material so that you make as few cuts as possible. The boards are veneered on all edges, and obviously, taking an inch or two off a length will expose the chipboard. You can buy rolls of edging veneer to hide such edges, but it is best to avoid the situation if you can.

There will be times when boards have to be cut, and here it is wise to plan your design so that cut edges are hidden behind a sound surface. By far the best joint for this type of carpentry is the butt joint, so all your cuts must be accurate to form perfect right-angles.

Small pieces can be cut with a tenon saw; this will give the cleanest edge. For large boards, a fine-tooth hand saw is better. The best tool is a portable saw or a saw bench; the work will be much simplified, and you can ensure accuracy of cut.

Having got your butt joint, you have the problem of securing it. There are a number of possibilities. Special joints are supplied by the board makers, but up to the time of writing, we have not found one which gives a really satisfactory result. While they hold, they don't pull the parts tightly together and this is essential. You can buy special knock-down joints as used on some bought furniture, involving a pin and a slotted cam. These are very good, for the more you tighten, the tighter the joint. They are, of course, more expensive, and you must weigh up whether it is an advantage to have a knock-down unit.

Ordinary square section hardwood batten can be used to join two sections if you drill holes to go into each board. This method is fine except where items have to slide into a frame.

In this case you can use drilled aluminium angle. With both methods, it looks neater if you finish the batten or angle a couple of inches from the front of the frame.

If you want a completely invisible joint, you can dowel your joints, in which case you need a little dowelling jig so that holes are true. Used in conjunction with a good adhesive, very firm joints are possible. Remember to cut a vee-groove in the dowel so that glue can ooze out, or use ready-fluted dowels. Alternatively you can use screws, fitting a neat plastic dome over the head to give a decorative effect. If you can get hold of chipboard screws, use these, as they are specially designed to grip chipboard.

With all butt jointed frames, the main difficulty is in getting dead square results. Accurate cutting is the first essential, backed up by a really dead true piece of plywood or hardboard for a backing. This should be put on before the glue in the frame sets, and it will pull everything into true. The job is more complex where other pieces are included in a frame, such as divisions in a bookcase. Here it is essential to plan very carefully your order of assembly.

The first essential when designing your furniture is to plan to hide as many cut edges as you can by butting them against an adjoining piece of board, or by locating cut edges at the rear so that a plywood or hardboard back hides them. But there comes the time when you really are faced with a cut edge which has to be visible. What to do then? A colleague hit this snag recently when he designed a piano stool. He said he would shape it like the legs of the actual piano – a graceful curve. This meant that he had to cut his veneered chipboard, exposing bare edges everywhere except on the top of the board!

The first important thing is to cut the board cleanly, with the cut at right angles to the board so you get a dead square edge. Our friend used a Wolf jig saw attachment fitted to a multi-speed power tool set on high speed (2,400 revs). It gave a very neat cut. It is important to keep the blade moving on tight curves to avoid a rough edge. And the board has to be well anchored to avoid judder. One way is to nail the board to spare pieces of rough timber, nailing through waste areas.

A final smooth over with fine glasspaper is all that is needed, then over to the edging. You can get two types of edging veneer for veneered chipboards. The first type has a dry adhesive

MATERIALS, TOOLS AND SECURITY

backing, the adhesive being activated by heat. The second has a release paper on the back; peel off the paper and the veneer is ready for attaching.

Clamp the work firmly so that you can press hard on an edge without it moving. For the hot version you need your wife's best iron, set at a medium temperature, and you are in business. Start at a point which will be hidden when the furniture is in sight if you intend going right around the piece. This means that your joint will be hidden if it is not too good. If you just have one edge to cover, then the job is easier.

Hold the edging strip in place and try it along the length so you are sure the strip is not wandering. Then apply the hot iron base to the strip and slowly move along. The adhesive quickly softens and grips rather like hot chewing gum. It is necessary to stop ironing and press the stuck strip firmly in place – perhaps with an old flat iron – to make sure the strip is home. More important, it takes the heat out of the veneer, hardening up the adhesive immediately.

Curves are easy to tackle, though with tight ones you must go easy or you will crack the wood across the grain. A right angle is not possible, so if you must turn a sharp corner, cut off your veneer with a razor blade and start again.

You will find the veneer is a shade wider than necessary, so when the edge is cold, carefully trim away the surplus with a razor blade or chisel. Watch the wood grain, for sometimes it tries to guide the blade into the chipboard. If this happens, simply start at the other end. Finally, rub all edges very gently with a fine grade glasspaper wrapped around a block of wood or cork.

You will find that the whole veneer is strengthened when you apply your finish. Three coats of a polyurethane seal will make the job really tough. Should you have a gap or two, before sealing, fill them with matching Brummer stopping. Allow to dry then rub smooth.

STANDARD JOINERY

Handymen could make more use of standard joinery units as produced by our first-class joinery manufacturers and a closer study of their catalogues would show that there are many jobs that could be tackled which, perhaps, at first seemed outside the handyman's province. A few examples follow.

Assume you want to build an extension on to your house to your own design. You can buy curtain wall units of framing filled in with tongued and grooved cedar boards and with hardwood sills ready fitted. Then you could plan to use standard window frames with a practically unlimited variety of opening casements. And you can buy a ready-made external door frame complete with sill, plus any one of a dozen designs of external door to go in the hole.

We are not suggesting that you could finish the job with standard units, but much of the basic constructional work can be done for you by expert joiners.

Windows available vary from a simple narrow unit about 50 cm wide through to square, semi-circular or angled bays up to about 3 m wide. Pivot windows or reversible double-glazed windows are available, too, if you want something a little more elaborate.

Door patterns vary considerably from plain flush veneered doors for internal use through to panelled doors for glazing or firecheck doors for doorways leading to a garage. There is a wide range of garage doors for either hinge operation or for up-and-over use. You can get door frames in which to hang them.

Perhaps you want to fit out your kitchen with units. Well, by all means buy whitewood units or prepared units from your furniture store, but it is worth examining the comprehensive range of standard stock units carried by the joinery manufacturer. You can get sink units in a pack, ready for assembly complete with all fittings, and there are standard cupboard units both for wall mounting and floor standing.

How about a new staircase? These are made to standard specification too – or you can have something special made up to your own requirements. Balustrading and panelling can be supplied loose to order.

So, if you want to put in a picture window or a bullseye window, hang a new garden gate or replace a garage door, get hold of a joinery catalogue and see if there is something there to suit. And when it comes to dressing up your joinery, you will find a varied selection of hardware, from latches and locks to catches and letterplates.

GLASS AND GLAZING

It is a funny thing that very often the chap who is willing to

MATERIALS, TOOLS AND SECURITY

tackle almost any D.I.Y. job will fight shy of glass cutting. Yet there is very little to it apart from confidence and a good wheel cutter. There are more elaborate cutters such as diamond cutters, but these are best left to the tradesmen.

Let us see how a piece of glass is cut. The first essential is to see that the glass is perfectly clean, for you will never cut dirty glass. Then you need a good base on which to cut it. A table with an old piece of blanket spread on it is ideal, and it is a good tip to spread a newspaper over the blanket as the rules between the columns are excellent guide lines. Oil the cutting wheel with paraffin. Lay the glass on the prepared base and mark where your cut is to be made. A lot of fuss is made about holding the cutter. Most important is to hold it firmly and comfortably. It is not necessary to copy the tradesman's hold. A pen grip can be used provided the cutter is held upright.

Lay a straight-edge along the line, then press the cutter against it at the farthest point from you. Press on the cutter and draw it towards you so that the wheel whispers across the glass. Don't press too hard or you will only splinter the glass surface. Press too lightly and the glass will not be cut at all. It is getting this right pressure which calls for practice. It is important to run the cutter off the edge of the glass at the end of the cut.

With a clear line made, lay a matchstick under the cut at each end of the glass and press down either side. The cut will run and you will get a clean division. Smaller pieces can be separated merely by holding the glass in your hands, thumbs on top and fingers bunched underneath. Twist the wrists apart and the glass will break. To remove very fine slivers, you can nibble the glass away using the square cut-outs on the side of the cutter.

Now what about the glass? There are very many types available in an interesting range of patterns. For normal window work where the window is not much above 3 ft. by 3 ft., 24 oz. glass is adequate (glass is specified by weight per square foot). For larger windows use 32 oz. The really large picture windows and glass shelving need $\frac{1}{4}$ in. thick plate glass.

When cutting (or ordering) glass to replace a broken pane, measure the frame carefully and see that it is square. Then deduct $\frac{1}{8}$ in. from both dimensions to allow for easy fit in the frame. When the frame has been cleaned out, a bed of putty should be placed in the rebate, and the glass is pressed on to this so that the putty squeezes out around the edges. This cushions the glass, and makes a watertight seal.

Always press the glass in place from the edges, *never* from the middle. If you have a textured glass, fit it with the texture on the inside. Hold the glass in place with a few fine pins or glazing sprigs tapped in with a chisel. Keep the chisel in contact with the glass and slide it into contact with the pin. In this way there is no danger of cracking the glass. You can then apply the final bead of putty.

LUBRICATION

Oil or grease can do a number of things. It can prevent rust and corrosion; it can certainly make things work more easily, and it can eliminate those irritating noises some folk seem deaf to.

Hand tools benefit from a regular thin coating of oil on metal parts, especially during winter months. It is a good idea to have a stick with a lump of thick felt tied to it which is kept permanently standing in a drop of oil in a jar. It doesn't take a second to give tool blades a wipe over after use, and they will keep in tip-top condition.

Give mechanical parts a good coating of grease before storing away. Items such as the lawnmower will stay like new under a

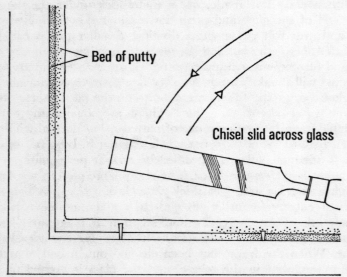

Using a chisel to tap glazing sprigs into place

MATERIALS, TOOLS AND SECURITY

layer of grease, and it doesn't take long to wipe it off when the mower is needed again.

Spots that are awkward to get at can be coated with oil using an aerosol pack, though bear in mind that thin oils evaporate fairly quickly.

For garden gates use a lump of grease. Graphite grease is ideal as it is a very persistent material and an excellent lubricant; but it is pretty mucky stuff, so be sure to wipe off any surplus or your children will find it!

Most folk lubricate locks incorrectly. Don't use oil as it only attracts dust which can cause things to jam up. If you must use any oil, put the smallest drop on the key and turn it a few times. Far better to invest in a graphite puffer pack and puff the dust into the mechanism. This will work well and will not attract dust. Graphite grease is ideal for padlocks which must be left outside. Again, a little applied to the key will lubricate the wards.

Oil is very much a waste of time with most hinges, again due to evaporation. Far better use a little clear lubricant such as Vaseline.

Wood can be lubricated, too. Use a stub of a candle on drawer runners, and you will be amazed at the difference. Another good timber lubricant is French chalk or baby talcum powder. If you have squeaky floorboards, and you think the cause is boards rubbing together, puff plenty of talc down the gaps until the noise stops. The same applies to squeaky stairs.

By the way, oil does affect rubber, so if a moving joint where rubber is present needs lubricating, use graphite dust or special rubber lubricant.

AEROSOLS AND PAD BRUSHES

There are ways of painting these days other than using the good old standard paint brush. The aerosol can, for example.

In 1950 the sale of aerosols in this country was 50,000; in 1969 it was 253 million – and by 1975 it is estimated the figure will be over 500 million – eight per head of population! Not all are paint of course, but the paint can has steadily been increasing in popularity, and now you can get just about everything from best quality polyurethane to galvanizing; clear varnish to the brightest of glosses.

Let's look at the advantages first. The aerosol is very easy to use; it gives a smooth, brush-free finish and it is usually designed to dry quickly, allowing a second coat to be applied within a very short time. There are no brushes to clean out afterwards, with a saving on cleaners. It is ideal on surfaces such as wickerwork or wrought ironwork, and it can apply protective finishes to areas you may not even be able to reach with a bristle brush. You can swap from one colour to another just by picking up another can.

The secret of successful application is to use the aerosol as you would any good spray gun, and apply coats thinly – and as many as necessary to give good coverage. Most amateurs ruin the job by putting too much on at once, and the paint sags or runs. A steady build-up is always the answer, working only at the recommended distance.

It pays to up-end the can after painting, press the nozzle until only gas comes out and so clear the jet. Failure to do this can result in blotchy, spattered results. Don't worry about waste of gas. There is more in the can than you will ever need.

Well, are there any snags with aerosols? There can be if you are not aware of their limitations. Let's look at one or two. First, the aerosol is not really suited to large jobs. It is a large can that will do a door, for example. With the smaller cans you may need up to three, and the snag is you don't know when the paint is going to run out, or if the next one will match the last – if you thought to buy a spare. It helps a bit now that many containers state roughly how much coverage you will get, but of course this is only a guide. Secondly, you do pay for the convenience of the aerosol, but for many jobs this is money well spent.

Then there is the problem of paint mist. There are jobs where the convenience of the aerosol would be lost through having to carefully mask a surface. And do be careful when spraying black paint in the garden when the wind is blowing towards the next door neighbour's white car!

In fairness, there are often unnecessary fears. Aerosols just don't explode if treated properly. They are very thoroughly tested with plenty of safety margin. But do bear in mind the precautions. Don't subject the container to excessive heat. Don't throw the can on a fire. Don't spray in a room where there is a naked flame – or gas or electric fire in use. Have adequate

MATERIALS, TOOLS AND SECURITY

ventilation. Don't mess about with empty cans, puncturing them.

Well, where do we go from here? You can buy independent packs of gas which can be used in conjunction with a container of paint. This means that one aerosol can be used for an indefinite number of colours. And there are pistol grips to make holding larger cans a more comfortable business.

The spray has come to stay, but as a footnote, let us say that the brush is not obsolete. The latest type of brush, called the pad brush, has a great future. The trouble is, we are so conservative as to make its introduction a slow process. It consists of a mohair rectangle mounted on a foam plastic pad, which in turn is fixed to a handle, or grip.

If you have never used a pad brush, at least give one a try. For large areas, it is ideal, applying paint evenly and smoothly at a very rapid rate. Pad brushes are best used with emulsion paint, as this washes out easily. If you intend using oil-base paints, ask whether the foam and adhesive will stand up to

PAINT PADS

Work in all directions

Paint pads – the new and efficient way of painting

modern brush cleaners. If not, you will have to use turps, or paraffin, to clean the mohair. We also find the pad brush excellent for ceiling work. No drips, and no spatter as you get with some rollers. Give one a try.

ADHESIVES

Not so many years ago, the types of adhesive could be numbered on one hand, and everyone knew what they were used for. Now the types literally run into hundreds – and few folk know which is used for what.

We are often asked what is the difference between a glue and an adhesive. Today, both terms are used loosely. At one time a glue was connected with products made from animals, while adhesive referred to products artificially made. Further than that, don't worry. They all stick.

Remember that no adhesive has universal application, so be sure you choose the right material for the job in hand. Be very wary of those adhesives which are said to 'stick anything to everything'. If this were possible, so many types would not have been developed.

Animal glue is still in common use. Made from bones, fish and other animal products, it offers a cheap means of fixing wood joints or sticking cardboard. Hot glues provide the best joint as the liquid percolates the wood fibres. Tubes of animal glue, used cold, are usually associated with handicrafts. This type of glue is not suitable for woodwork exposed to damp, as the glue softens and melts when wet.

To deal with situations where damp is present, choose a synthetic resin adhesive. The adhesive is supplied in two parts, which have to be mixed before the adhesive will set. Setting is by chemical action, and once started, neither damp nor lack of air will affect the setting. Warmth will shorten setting time.

Epoxy resin adhesive, supplied in small tubes, is ideal for repairs to china, glass and metal. The joint, once set, is unaffected by boiling water or household chemicals. Be warned. Don't mix more than you need. The rest is sheer waste, as you cannot keep it. And don't let one tube contaminate the other, or you will lose the lot!

P.V.A. adhesives are now freely available, in varying quantities. They are milky-white in colour, odourless and dry almost transparent. P.V.A. is now widely used for paper and

MATERIALS, TOOLS AND SECURITY

card sticking, and for woodwork, but it has little resistance to damp or heat. It is the adhesive which can be used in a concrete mix to give the concrete adhesive properties, to stop it dusting and flaking, and to allow you to feather-edge your work.

Casein glue, as its name suggests, is made from skimmed milk. It is popular for woodwork, withstanding damp to a limited extent, but not enough for it to be used outdoors. It is also widely used for bonding flooring materials to the floor. Supplied as a powder, water is added as necessary.

Rubber-base adhesives score over all those mentioned in that they form flexible bonds, whereas all the others will crack when flexed. But rubber-base adhesives do not give the mechanical strength, so they are not recommended for woodworking joints. They are ideal for sticking down sheet materials such as laminated plastic.

Various types of rubber adhesive are available for jobs varying from carpet repairs to sticking tiles on walls. Be sure to choose the right one. And take a tip and buy some solvent for cleaning. Some of these adhesives stick tighter than skin!

Solvent-based adhesives are available for such specialist materials as P.V.C. and polystyrene. They do in fact bond by dissolving the surface of the plastic. Such adhesives are used for model kits and for repairs to plastic macs.

Cellulose and starch adhesives are familiar to the amateur paperhanger. The cellulose type is noted for its non-staining properties, but it has a very high water content. Starch pastes may mark if care is not taken, but they have far lower water content, making them better suited to heavy papers.

Most of the glues and adhesives mentioned are best left under slight pressure while the adhesive sets. Use cramps, strips of Sellotape, strong elastic bands, or strips cut from old inner tubes and used as bandages.

The big advantage of the impact type adhesive is that the bond is immediate. Both surfaces should be coated with a thin layer of adhesive allowed to get touch dry, then the two surfaces are pressed together. Positioning is important, especially when tackling such jobs as covering a table with laminated plastic. Use a sheet of brown paper or, better still, siliconised paper (such as that which backs Fablon or Con-Tact) between the two glue surfaces, position the plastic, then pull out the paper.

Never use too much of any adhesive, thinking it will make a

BEGINNER'S GUIDE TO DO-IT-YOURSELF

joint that much stronger – it won't. A little in the right place is plenty. And, finally, don't try to stick polythene with adhesive. As far as we know there isn't one which will. Adhesive tape does pretty well, but the best joins are made by heat sealing.

TOOLS FOR D.I.Y.

Here is a selection of general tools for use in and around the house. The basic ones will be found of use on nearly every job tackled; others can be bought as required. Do select your tools with care. Some may seem expensive, but they will give good service and, when considered over a period of years they are good value for money.

Steel rule
Steel tape
Try square (for accurately marking right angles)
Pencil
Crosscut saw (*may* not be needed if power saw available)
Tenon saw (again, may not be required)
Hacksaw (for cutting metals and tough compositions)
Throwaway blade plane
Hand drill (for use with twist drills)
Set of twist drills
Small and large screwdrivers
Pincers
Pliers
Cross-pein hammer, about $\frac{1}{2}$ lb.
Selection of wood chisels, preferably bevel edge
Chain wrench (for gripping large, circular or irregular objects)
Oilstone, with two different grade sides
Countersink bit
Masonry drills (Nos. 8 and 10) or jumpers
Multi-blade knife
Self-grip wrench
Nail punch
Spirit level
Claw hammer
Club hammer (for heavy work)
Cold chisel (for masonry cutting)
Glasscutter
Electric drill, preferably two-speed

Disc sander
Circular saw
Jig saw
Impact attachment (for drilling into hard masonry materials)

TOOL HIRE

There is nothing new about the hire business. Tradesmen have been hiring equipment for years, but it is only fairly recently that a real effort has been made to attract the keen handyman to hire equipment, too. Now there are a number of first rate firms who can supply quality equipment, regularly maintained and serviced, to help with just about every job you can think of. Their charges are reasonable, and the modest deposit is usually returned within a few days of the equipment being taken back to the hirer.

With many of us, time is an important factor. And this is where it can pay you to hire. For example, faced with the prospect of chipping cardboard-like paper from a 22 ft. by 10 ft. lounge, Tony Wilkins hired a Sanderson steam wallpaper stripping machine operated by Calor gas. The lounge resembled a steam laundry, but the whole room was clear of paper in three hours! It cost a couple of pounds, but he was spared hours of hard slog.

There is practically no limit to the items you can hire. To save yourself money, do all the preparation work before you collect the tool you need. For example, clear the room and punch down all nail heads before taking delivery of a floor sander. Do collect the appliance yourself, if possible. While a hire company will deliver and collect, it will cost you more money.

How about a bit of exterior decorating? You can get extending ladders to which you can add brackets to take scaffold planks. Or perhaps you prefer a tower scaffold. Various heights are available, but one up to 12 ft. is usual.

For tough work you can get a Kangol hammer; for concrete mixing an electrically operated concrete mixer. Then there's spray equipment, floor sanders, equipment and tools for installing central heating, damp-proof course injection machines, garden tools, chain saws, car maintenance equipment (hoists, gear pullers and panel beating sets) and kits to tackle woodworm in the loft.

BEGINNER'S GUIDE TO DO-IT-YOURSELF

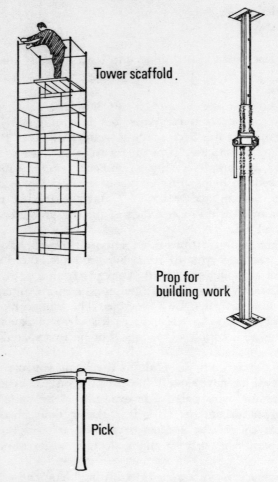

Tower scaffold.

Prop for building work

Pick

Don't think this is the end. There are hire firms that will supply catering equipment from urns to cake stands, bars and ice buckets. Camping equipment for the most ambitious holiday, marquees for garden parties plus coloured lights and bingo sets, too, if you wish! Typewriters, film shows, cine cameras and projectors, push chairs or roof racks. And, if you feel energetic, you can hire a removal van, and you can do that yourself, too!

SECURITY
It is sobering to think that at least one house in Britain, on

MATERIALS, TOOLS AND SECURITY

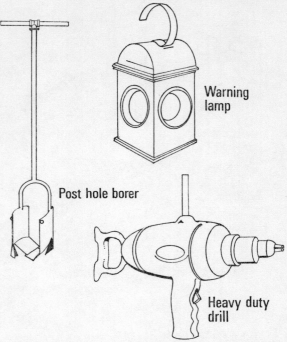

Warning lamp

Post hole borer

Heavy duty drill

average, is broken into every three minutes right around the clock and throughout the year. Who knows, if you present the opportunity, you may be next on the list!

Sheer apathy on the part of house owners seems to offer the greatest incentive to the intruder, when even the most elementary precautions could be enough to send a thief off for easier game. Let's have a look at some of the precautions you can take.

First, your doors. The normal spring lock is easy meat for the burglar, even without a key. Fit a good mortice deadlock with at least five levers. This will resist most attacks including attempt to hacksaw through the bolt. Back this up with a sliding bolt top and bottom of the door, using the longest screws you can to secure them. The big failing of many small bolts is that the screws you must use are so fine that even a hard push would wrench the bolt from the door.

If you prefer, you can fit a security bolt to the door instead of the sliding bolt. This is operated by a special key, and the bolt cannot be pushed back when the key is withdrawn. This type of bolt is particularly useful in doors with glass panels, for

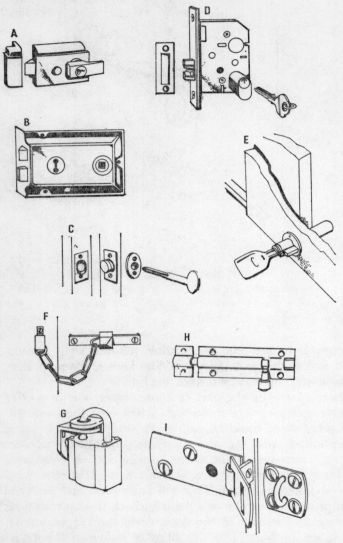

A selection of security devices. A. Automatic deadlocking nightlatch. B. Rim Lock. C. Mortise security bolt. D. Cylinder mortise lock for sliding door. E. Sliding door lock. F. Safety chain set. G. Window lock with padlock. H. Barrel bolt. I. Clam hasp and staple. J. Upright mortise lock. K. Key-in-knob cylindrical lockset. L. General purpose mortise latch

MATERIALS, TOOLS AND SECURITY

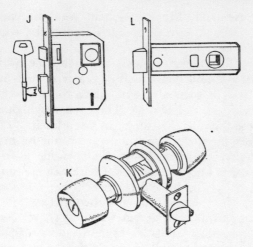

even if a panel is broken, the bolt cannot be released.

The bolder burglar may even knock on the door if he is pretty sure you are alone. There are two precautions you can take here. Fit a door viewer, which gives you a wide angle view of your visitors without being seen from inside. Couple this with a good porch light so that your doorway is well lit at night. Any thief or thug prefers to operate in the dark.

Fit a good door chain which allows the door to be partially opened; but the door must be closed again before the security chain can be released. If in doubt, don't let him in! The door viewer usually needs only a ½ in. hole through the door, and the door chain is fixed by means of screws.

The next weak points are of course the windows, and especially those out of view of neighbours. Be sure to close all downstairs windows securely before you go to bed. Back up the normal fittings by a suitable security device. For sash windows, there is a special key-operated screw bolt which will lock both sashes together. If you want a sash to remain open for ventilation purposes, you can fit what is called an acorn stop. This allows a sash to move a little way, then it checks any further movement. The usual catch on sash windows can be released by a knife blade or a strip of celluloid, and to counter this you can fit a Fitch catch which cannot be moved once locked.

For casement windows, there are small key-operated security

67

bolts and screw bolts. Metal casement windows can be fitted with special locks. A turn of a catch secures the window, and unlocking is by key.

Various audible alarm systems are available which, when wired to windows and doors, will give a noisy welcome to any intruder. If you fit such a system, place the bell where it will be heard clearly by neighbours. Then tell neighbours and the police that it is there so that they can listen for it.

For old folk on their own, more use could be made of the intercom telephone systems now available for a few pounds. These are battery operated, and the wire can be run from one flat to another so that an elderly person can summon help, if needed, merely by pressing a button, then talking.

You can buy drawer locks, but when away, we consider that it is better to remove valuables from the house, then leave all drawers and wardrobes unlocked. A thief working at leisure while you are away will smash open any locked drawers and cupboards, adding to the trail of damage.

Don't leave ladders around. They offer easy access to upstairs open windows. If you go away, stop the tradesmen calling and get a neighbour to push things through your letterbox if they are left sticking out.

Check the credentials of strangers wishing to enter your house. If in doubt, don't let them in.

Then, keep your eyes and ears open for a stranger peering in next door's windows; the tinkle of glass behind a neighbour's house when you know they are away; a light where there should not be one; folk sitting in a car obviously keeping watch on a house. Phone the police or quietly call on a neighbour who has a phone. The police are there to help you day and night, but many thieves get away scot-free because the police are not informed soon enough.

When you go away for a while, do what you can to disguise the fact. A light or two left on is a deterrent, and you can use the time clock of an electric blanket to put on a standard lamp and table lamp for a few hours in the evenings. If you do this, inform your neighbours, or you will have the police around!

It is interesting to note that double glazing is a deterrent to the crook who usually breaks a window and releases a catch. And a Venetian blind is not easy to contend with when down.

MATERIALS, TOOLS AND SECURITY

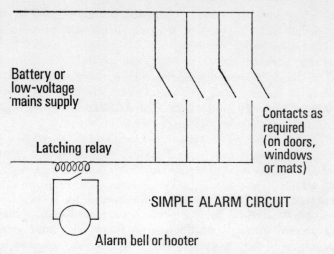

A simple circuit for a burglar alarm – any number of contacts can be added

Having taken the necessary precautions, sleep soundly. If your house is difficult to enter, the thief will go elsewhere. He doesn't wish to waste time or draw attention to himself, and he can always be sure that just down the road there is someone silly enough to allow him easy entry.

CHAPTER FOUR
Repairs and Jobs Inside the House

WALL TILES

There are many ways you can tile a wall. A good imitation tiling can be created by using plastic-face hardboard which has been pressed during manufacture to form 'tiles' and grouting. You can buy this in panels or easily handled squares, and it offers an economical way of tackling large areas.

Moulded polystyrene tiles (not to be confused with expanded polystyrene used for ceiling tiles) can also be used. The polystyrene tile has a pearly sparkle, it is easy to fix and keep clean, but you must be careful as it can be scratched. Then there are thin P.V.C. sheets moulded to look like tiles; these sheets are backed with adhesive and a protective backing paper. These look least like tiles, but they offer a very light, easy to apply method for those who want quick results.

It is not so very long ago that using ceramic tiles was a job for the expert. The tiles were thick and heavy, and they had to be set in a cement mortar. But the introduction of thin, $4\frac{1}{4}$ in. square tiles has changed all that. This, plus the introduction of new adhesives with which the tiles can be fixed to the wall, makes applying modern ceramic tiles extremely easy. Another point of interest is that colours and sizes are standard, so you need buy only what you can afford. Then, at a later date, you can buy some more and continue, knowing that the new tiles will match the old perfectly.

As the tiles are light, you can tile to just about any clean, dry surface. That includes plaster, hardboard, and even old tiled surfaces that are sound enough to cover over.

Most tiles have small spacing nibs moulded with the tile, and these automatically provide the correct grouting gap as the tiles are positioned. With plain tiles you put small pieces of card between the edges as spacers. These are removed prior to grouting.

Now let us have a look at the actual laying process. Few tools are needed. A tile cutter – of either the wheel type as used for cutting glass, or the tungsten carbide tipped type. Then you need a straight wood batten, a spirit level, adhesive, grouting powder and, of course, the tiles.

To calculate how many tiles you need, it is a good idea to get a length of batten, and make marks on it at intervals of $4\frac{5}{16}$ in. This is the width of a tile plus the gap for grouting. Use the batten to count how many tiles are needed vertically and horizontally over the area to be covered, multiply the figures together, and this is how many tiles you need. There are special round edge and corner tiles, and these should be allowed for in your calculations.

With tiling, the secret of success is to get your first row dead level and true. So don't be tempted to use a skirting board as your base. It may be uneven, and, if it is, all your tiling will follow it. Measure up from the skirting board one tile and space width ($4\frac{5}{16}$ in.) and make a mark. Line your lath on this and, using the spirit level, make a true horizontal line. Now secure the batten to the wall with masonry nails, with its top edge along the marked line. You can tile up from this.

If you are working from the floor, and the floor is really irregular, set the true line $\frac{1}{4}$ in. higher still. This will leave an irregular gap at the bottom of your tiling which can be hidden behind a strip of quadrant moulding. Of course, you can tile direct up from a new working top, or the top of a basin or sink. But do be sure the surface is horizontal.

With your batten in place, apply adhesive. This is done using a notched spreader. Don't do too much at a time – about a square yard is right. Apply the tiles by putting one edge in place, then allowing the tile to contact the wall. Never slide a tile in place or you will force adhesive up between tiles. Keep the gaps constant.

Cutting tiles is very easy. Mark the tile where it needs cutting, score it with a firm stroke of the tile cutter. Place the tile on a flat surface, decorative side up (which means scored side up) and place a matchstick under each end of the tile, directly under the score. Press firmly on either side of the score, and the tile will break cleanly. The Oporto tile cutter makes the job even easier.

Now how about cutting shapes? This is easy too. Get a tile file from your local D.I.Y. shop or tool shop. This fits in a fretsaw frame, and with it you can cut any shape quickly and neatly – as you would when fretsawing.

When the area has been tiled, leave the batten in place for 24 hours. To remove it earlier may allow the tiles to slide under the weight of those above. Then, with the batten removed, fill in the bottom row, trimming tiles where necessary.

Grouting is best done about 12 hours after tiling. Mix the powder as directed on the packet, then force it into the cracks with either a piece of damp rag or a small piece of sponge. Remove surplus grouting with a sponge, then leave it to set. Then give a final polish with a dry duster, and you will be amazed at the gleaming result.

You needn't stick to plain colours. There are a lot of patterned and hand painted tiles which can be used at random to break up a plain surface. And you can get items such as soap dish, toilet roll holder and towel rail all designed to fit in with the tiles.

DEALING WITH OLD OR DAMAGED CEILINGS

Decorating a ceiling is usually a fairly arm-aching job, but what if the ceiling is in pretty poor shape into the bargain? Most trouble occurs in older property where the ceilings are constructed of lath and plaster. If the keying fails, then you may have a ceiling which sags in places. You can test the ceiling by standing on a chair and pressing up on the ceiling. If a bulge can be pressed up, then the keying has failed. Unless cracking is bad, you can usually make a repair in the following manner.

Locate the position of the joists. The easiest way to do this is from the room above. Note the nail positions in the floorboards and measure to locate their position in relation to the ceiling below. Or, if you can lift a board, drill a fine hole through the ceiling near to a joist. Now use fairly long aluminium alloy or other rustless screws and screw up through the plaster and into the joists. The plaster will be forced back into place. Don't be tempted to use nails on ceiling work. You could well end up with the plaster about your ears!

If the area of loose plaster is badly cracked, it is best to pull it away. Hold a dust pan near to collect the mess. Brush out the loose dust and dirt. Then you need a key – or grip – for the new plaster. You can form this by screwing a number of rustless screws into the exposed woodwork, leaving the heads proud. You can now replaster the hole with a proprietary filler, but if the area is considerable, use Keene's cement, which is much cheaper and just as effective.

Rake out all cracks and gaps, and fill with a proprietary filler. Modern materials don't need an undercut crack very often, but it is a good idea to slightly open up the crack. Then there is no chance of the filler working loose.

If the lath and plaster is in pretty poor shape, as it has been in so many houses that were shaken up in the last war, then the best thing to do is get rid of the lot. This is a messy job. It is a good idea to give the ceiling a really good wetting before you start. This will reduce the filthy white dust that otherwise finds its way all over the house regardless of shut doors.

Rip away the laths and remove all nails. An excellent material to recover the ceiling is sheet plasterboard from which most modern ceilings are made. This is not an expensive material and it is relatively easy to fix. You can get full details from British Gypsum Ltd., Ferguson House, 15–17 Marylebone Road, London, N.W.1. If you prefer to work with one of the fibre building boards, drop a line to FIDOR, Stafford House, Norfolk Street, London, W.C.2. They will be pleased to advise you.

With new materials, you may have to lay new battens across the joists and, perhaps, battens the other way so that boards or squares are supported on all four edges. Hiding joints is a bit of a problem, but manufacturers will advise you. Some may be covered with a cotton scrim or a special paper tape. Then when you line the ceiling with a lining paper the joints will be invisible.

If you want an olde worlde look, you can batten between the joists, then fill in so that the under-face of each joist is left showing. If stained and treated with a seal, they can look quite attractive.

If you don't want to paper a new ceiling, you may care to paint it with one of the plastic paints such as Selftex. This is a thick paint, not to be confused with emulsion paint. It is put on thick, and is then given a texture by running a decorator's comb over it, by just pulling up the surface into blobs with a wood float or stippling with bunched paper or plastic. The idea is that the texture hides minor irregularities, nails and joints. It is widely used on new estates.

There is only one snag with this material. You are stuck with a texture for keeps. The surface is very hard to remove without a special steam stripper, and you can easily damage the plasterboard underneath.

A simple way of giving a new look to a sound but cracked and stained ceiling is to cover the old plaster with expanded polystyrene tiles. These are easily fitted with adhesive, and they can be had in a variety of textures. Just make sure you get them dead square. And if you want to paint them, do so with emulsion paint before you put them up. Much easier this way.

A final word. If you have a hanging flex in the dead centre of the room and wish to vary the lighting arrangements, why not reroute the wiring if you have to have the ceiling down? This is the obvious time to do it.

COVE CORNICE

Cove cornice, which can be of expanded polystyrene, plaster, fibre or even plastic, adds a neat finish between the wall and the ceiling, where sometimes unsightly cracks appear. Apart from appearance, it effectively hides that joint between walls and ceiling where cracks so often appear. These cracks are quite normal, for with even slight house movement between summer and winter, this movement must show itself.

The first essential when applying cove is to clean off the surfaces where it has to be fixed. This means scraping off wallpaper or paint down to the bare plaster. Old distemper is the worst possible base, so this must be scrubbed off. Then, with the plaster clean, scraping – or hatching – with a trowel tip will add a little roughness to afford a grip. Redecorating time is best for this job, when the walls have been stripped and before any new decoration is applied.

Expanded polystyrene cove is the simplest to use because it is so light, but it gives the least attractive result. About 3 ft. is the longest length you can buy, so you need a number of joints – which are extremely hard to disguise! One manufacturer advises you to taper down the ends and overlap them, but this adds to the expense because of the overlap. We think the best way is to butt the ends; pare off any slight differences in height with a razor blade, then rub cellulose filler into the joint with the fingers. On no account use glasspaper! It doesn't smooth the stuff; it merely roughs it up.

Internal and external angle pieces to match are supplied, which ensures neat turns. Fixing, by the way, is by special adhesive. Many normal adhesives attack the foam plastic, with quite dramatic results!

An alternative material is Anaglypta cove cornice, available from most shops stocking Crown wallpapers. This is supplied by the roll, and it resembles whitish moulded cardboard. One advantage is that a whole wall can be tackled in one length, so you get no ugly joints. Corners, internal and external, must be cut using a paper template supplied.

Dextrine adhesive is used for fixing, and it is quite tricky getting the length up until you get the knack. The cove must be held temporarily with fine panel pins just until the glue hardens. Full instructions are supplied with every roll. The only disadvantage of this material is that it fits almost flat to the wall and ceiling at its edges, so you get no step to paper up to.

The most effective cove is, in our opinion, Gypsum cove. The plaster has a tough paper covering, and again, you can buy the cove in lengths long enough to cover most runs in one go, so there are no joints. Corners have to be cut using the template provided, and it is as well to get a bit of practice in on this before you make your first serious cut. Should you make a mistake, you are then lumbered with a bit perhaps 12 ft. long which isn't long enough for you to have another go without patching. Once you get the knack, it is dead easy; even so, measure twice, cut once.

A special plaster adhesive is supplied for this job, and, provided the wall is prepared correctly, the quite heavy cove can be offered up to the ceiling, pressed in place and there it will stay! No nails or supports. Incidentally, you will certainly need an extra pair of hands to help you handle the long lengths.

A word of general advice. If you encounter a wavy ceiling – and this is often the case with bedrooms – don't try to push the cove, whatever the type, into the hollows. Let it find its own level line, then fill in above with filler. This way the error will be hidden rather than highlighted. Here again is the advantage of the long length, for this will hide the irregularities.

When you come to painting, expanded polystyrene will take

paint, but will retain a slight open textured appearance which isn't unpleasant. Anaglypta cove should be primed before painting with a normal oil-base primer, even if you plan to emulsion over it. This is to avoid the water in water-base paints expanding the cove, perhaps causing wrinkles. The gypsum base cove can be painted with an oil or water-base system.

One final point; gypsum materials are available in a number of lengths. Consider carefully before you order what lengths are economical, and whether they can be manoeuvred upstairs.

FINISHING WHITEWOOD

Whitewood furniture is not as cheap as it used to be – but it does offer you the advantage of finishing your furniture just as you want it. If you buy a good brand, you will find the quality high and the surface easy to decorate, but many of the cheaper makes use a sort of fluffy plywood which is practically impossible to paint.

You will find there are two basic types of whitewood. First there is the true whitewood which is intended to be painted. Then there is the furniture finished with a good top veneer, designed to be natural finished. We will look at both types; the type to be painted first.

Before you buy, decide what you want the furniture to look like. If you favour something decorative with a period flavour, you can get decorative mouldings in traditional designs which can be pinned or stuck in place prior to painting. These look a bit odd when first applied, but once painted, they can look very attractive.

If mouldings are not for you, yet you still prefer something decorative, have a look at the considerable range of transfers. You can get anything from neat floral posies through to cartoon characters. Then there are Austrian-style patterned strips, and with these, your furniture could look really gay, for any room from kitchen to nursery. Decide this first, as your choice of decor can govern what you buy.

When you get your piece of whitewood, give it a good smooth down with a fairly fine glasspaper wrapped around a block. Work only with the grain of the wood, or you may produce deep scratches which you won't be able to eliminate. If you find minute cracks between joints, fill them with cellulose filler or a stopping, then rub smooth.

Now apply a thinnish primer to seal the pores of the wood and to provide a key for undercoat. When dry, apply undercoat, brushing it out well. When this is dry, you may well find that the wood feels rough to the touch, which means that the undercoat has lifted the grain slightly. Remove this roughness with a flour grade glasspaper, making sure you don't go through to the bare wood. Incidentally, we have never found it necessary to apply a three-coat system to the insides of items like wardrobes. Two coats of emulsion paint are usually sufficient. The first does raise the grain, but after a quick rub down, the second coat goes on well enough.

With the undercoat nice and smooth, it is a good idea to go over it with what is called a tack, or tacky, rag. This is a resin impregnated cloth which picks up all the fine dust off the unit, giving you a really clean surface.

Apply your top coat, brushing out well. This can be high gloss, eggshell, or matt, to suit your own requirements. If you choose a one-coat paint, you can omit the undercoat. If you have applied mouldings, these could be picked out in a contrasting colour, but they can look good in the same colour, leaving the play of light on the moulding to add character to the piece.

If you choose furniture with a decorative top veneer, rub down well as before, again making sure you work only with the wood grain. Now you have a choice of using an oil, a seal or a varnish. Oil gives a very flat sheen, and it darkens the wood slightly. A polyurethane seal, or vanish, gives more of a sheen, and the sheen turns to a gloss as additional coats are applied. Or you could use a home French polish or a high gloss lacquer.

You can darken the veneer by applying a wood stain before finishing, but take a tip from us and do some experimenting before you do much. The darkening can be deceptive. We have found that two or three coats of seal darkens the wood quite enough, and it brings out the grain pattern beautifully. If you feel the gloss you have produced is too high, don't worry, use fine steel wool lubricated with wet soap to take down the gloss. Or use matt polyurethane.

If painting whitewood doesn't appeal, you can now buy really good adhesive-backed veneers which you can apply yourself, using only a warm iron. Or there is another type which comes complete with adhesive. Or, if you want to be a little more ambitious, you can cover whitewood with laminated plastic sheet – and very good it can look too. Vinyl coated fabrics can be used to good effect, and you can get special adhesives to stick them on.

Finally, spend a bit of time choosing handles and other fittings. They can have quite an effect on the finished appearance. Most shops selling whitewood offer a good choice. Try not to buy cheap ones – especially lacquered metal ones. Nearly always they tarnish and look dreadful.

CLEANING OLD FURNITURE

There is many a bargain piece of furniture hidden under a covering of cracked varnish or grubby paint. And this applies particularly today with the revived interest in natural-finish woodwork. Having selected a piece which looks promising, check to see that all joints are sound and that no parts are damaged. If there are loose joints, it will pay to pull them apart, or persuade them with a rubber mallet. Then strip the old finish off before re-assembling. Broken sections can be glued before stripping so that the joint will be lost when smoothing down.

Remove all old paint or varnish with a chemical paint stripper. If necessary, apply two or three coats; don't try to get all the goo off in one go. A cabinet scraper or a Skarsten scraper used gently will help remove loosened material. Mouldings and carvings can be cleaned with wire wool. Don't rub too hard against wood grain or you will get scratches.

With the wood clean, rub down well with glasspaper, again working with the grain. Finish with a flour grade paper, and your wood will feel smooth and silky. If the timber is patchy in colour, or if it has obviously been stained dark, you can lighten it by using a wood bleach. Follow the instructions very carefully. After treatment, when dry, rub down with glasspaper until really smooth.

You now have a choice of finishes. Straight wax polishing satisfies some folk; or you can seal with a polyurethane seal. One coat merely seals the wood pores and brings out the grain pattern. A light rub over when hard, followed by a further one or two brush applied coats gives a pleasant sheen. If the sheen is too much, you can always flat it down again with fine wire wool.

Another method is to use one of the attractive transparent coloured varnishes. These are available in brilliant colours, and the effect is very pleasing.

If the wood is not attractive, you can always paint it, though this is a last resort. Apply primer first, smooth it when dry; dust off and apply undercoat and top coat. Take a tip and don't use a high gloss. An eggshell or matt finish looks far more classy. Or you can use an acrylic gloss which gives a sheen and needs no undercoat. Being water-based, you can rinse out brushes in water after use.

If you have a piece which is painted and the paint is in good condition, you don't need to strip it. Get a tin of abrasive paint cleaner – there is one called Trim. It removes grime and wax, and it will flat the old surface ready for repainting. Wash off the cleaner; allow to dry, then you can repaint with two top coats.

There are other materials available to enhance your furniture. There are stains of many shades, allowing you to match in with existing pieces of furniture. If you use a stain, try it on an unseen part first to see if you like the colour. Some darken when dry or look different when covered with a sealing coat.

There are also special handyman French polishes; these are very easy to use. And there are tough, brush applied varnishes which give a very high gloss. With these it is a good idea to do a test piece to see if you like the effect before doing the lot.

Folk often ask should they avoid pieces of furniture which have obvious woodworm holes. Provided that the timber is basically sound and interesting, buy it just the same; but get an aerosol of woodworm killer at the same time and inject every hole you can find until liquid squirts from surrounding holes. Then you can either leave your holes visible, showing you have a real antique, or you can fill them with Brummer Stopping of a matching colour.

Finally, don't be put off by tatty seat covers. In most cases the seat can be pressed out of the chair frame, and the tacks holding the old cover in place on the underside of the seat can be prised off. If you are lucky, the seat will still have a thin fabric cover holding the padding in place, so all you need do is get some new material; stretch it over the seat; tack it firmly and tautly in place; trim and replace the seat. It will probably be a tighter fit with new material, but you can usually work it into place.

If the padding has given up, you can buy polyurethane foam fairly cheaply, and this makes an excellent padding for seats. Don't overtighten your cover when covering foam plastic, or you will distort the foam and end up with wrinkles in the cover.

SIMPLE SHELVING

The trouble with most shelving is that it needs holding up, and most brackets look a mess – unless the shelf is in the garage or workshop. There are, however, ways you can fix shelves with no visible means of support.

For the first method, all you need is a plank for the shelf itself and two pieces of mild steel rod about 6 in. long. Holes are drilled in the wall to accept the rod, leaving about $2\frac{1}{2}$ in. proud. Then matching holes are carefully drilled into the rear of the shelf. The shelf is pushed on to the rods – and that's all there is to it.

In the second method you will need the shelf plus a stout batten of timber, preferably of the same material and as long as the shelf itself. Glue and screw the top rear edge of the shelf to one edge of the batten. Then two recesses are cut in the back of the batten, and these are covered by keyhole plates. If you can recess the plates in too, this will be better still. Next you need to drill and plug the wall at the spot where the shelf is to be, then drive home screws until there is just enough head proud to press into each keyhole plate. Countersunk heads are best for this. You can add end pieces to finish off the shelf.

If you want a neat form of alcove shelving that can readily be dismantled, just cut as many shelves as you need so that they fit neatly into the alcove. For spacers, at the ends, use similar timber; each piece will be as long as the distance between the shelves. Build up from the floor – to the ceiling if you wish. For extra security, you can pin narrow battens to the undersides of the shelves, just to hold the spacers close to the walls. When cutting the shelves, remember that the alcove may vary in width from bottom to top as well as front to back.

Radiator shelves are useful both for ornaments and protection of decorations. These can be made easily. Support for the shelf is merely two shaped blocks, wedge-shape for a push fit down the back of the radiator, coming to rest where the wedge finishes. This governs the height of the shelf above the radiator. Allow it to be a bit on the tight side, as the wood will shrink a shade when in constant contact with a hot radiator.

Now screw the wedges to the rear underside of the shelf, close to the radiator bracket positions. Be sure to drill holes for screws to avoid splitting the wedges, and recess the screws into the shelf top so that the shelf can be covered with laminated plastic. Such a shelf is a good push fit in place, where it sticks fast – with no supports visible.

JOINTING METHODS
Craftsmen of old relied on cunning jointwork to hold their furniture together but the good old butt joint is suitable for most jobs today. This is particularly true now that the veneered chipboard is so popular for furniture making. Here are a few ideas.

Dowels: A butt joint can be secured by dowels, though without a guide it isn't easy to get them dead true. You can get a neat little dowelling jig for about 75p, and this will help considerably. Be sure you set the depth carefully so that you don't come out through the decorative face of your wood. And be sure to nick a vee along the dowel length so that excess glue can get out. Alternatively you can use serrated dowels which grip even better.

Fillets: A simple triangular or square fillet of wood glued and pinned or glued and screwed will hold a joint firm. If you use one of the veneered boards, use special chipboard screws which are designed to grip well without splitting.

Metal angle: Aluminium angle is ideal for fixing corners. Holes need to be drilled and countersunk for small screws, then make sure you choose screws that won't come through the decorative surface of your board. If the angle is cut a bit short, it won't be so prominent.

Plastic joints: With the introduction of the veneered boards, manufacturers have introduced small plastic joint pieces to make the job really simple. The joint consists of two sections, and half is screwed to each board, then the two pieces are mated and screwed together by means of a single screw. These joints are all right if you merely want to hold two pieces, perfectly matched, together. But they will not pull parts together.

Knock-down fittings: These are used mostly by the trade. These are in two pieces (metal) which are mounted as for plastic joints. Applying a screwdriver to a captive screw engages the two parts and pulls them tight together by cam action. These are ideal for items of furniture you want to be able to dismantle quickly.

Glue and pin: Finally, don't despise the old glue and pin method. Modern glues are so good that usually the wood will break before the joint parts. Glue and pin is particularly suitable where a unit is backed with plywood or hardboard, for the backing will add considerably to the strength of the unit.

TIMBER TROUBLE

Nature's way of disposing of dead wood is to break it down by fungal and beetle attack. This you can see in action in any wood or forest. Unfortunately, Mother Nature doesn't discriminate between the dead trees in the wood, and the timber used in house construction, and given half a chance she will have a go at your home too!

Woodworm: Damage by woodworm already amounts to many millions of pounds a year, and the trouble is increasing every year, so it will pay you to examine your roof timbers, floors, and backs of furniture for tiny flight holes about $\frac{1}{12}$ in. in diameter. Actually, when you find these, the beetle has flown, but there may still be more at home.

The most common wood boring insect is the furniture beetle. The adult is about $\frac{1}{8}$ in. long, brown in colour, and it can fly well. The female lays about 60 eggs in rough wood or cracks between timbers, and after about three weeks the eggs hatch out and the grubs bore their way into the wood where they remain, chewing away and tunnelling below the surface, gradually weakening the structure. After about three years they emerge as fully grown beetles – and the cycle is repeated.

If you find small areas of attack, you can treat the timber by using an aerosol injector, and by applying a special insecticide by brush.

For a more severe attack, say in the loft, you would be wise to get a survey from a preservation company. Their survey is free, and there is no obligation to take their advice. But if you wish, they will quote for doing the job – and they will give you a guarantee against further attack for at least the next 20 years. But do note that the guarantee covers only the area actually treated – not other areas later attacked. If you prefer to do the job yourself, some hire firms can supply a suitable spray outfit – but follow their advice to the letter.

If you find trouble in furniture backs, treat the timber with an insecticidal fluid, paying particular attention to all cracks, and plain, untreated timber. You can buy a special insecticidal furniture polish which will also help to prevent trouble.

Longhorn beetles: A much more serious problem is the larger house longhorn beetle. If you have this one as a visitor, act fast – or he'll soon have the roof down!

Dry rot: This is an even more dangerous enemy. When timber has a moisture content of more than about 20 per cent, and ventilation is poor, the wood is just right for the millions of fungus spores in the air. These settle, and soon greyish strands spread through the timber. These destroy the timber, making it weak and brittle, and the fungus strands then move on to sound, dry timber, carrying their own water to raise the moisture content of the wood to the necessary level. The strands can penetrate brickwork and plaster, and the trouble can spread at an alarming rate.

Now how do you recognise dry rot? By a very musty smell, by timber warped and cracked across the wood grain, by its lack of resistance to the dig of a pen knife, and by signs of whitish strands and fungus growth on the underside of the timber. Again, specialist advice is recommended – and if you can afford it, have the trouble eliminated by experts. There are fluids you can use after cutting out every trace of damaged wood, and burning it, but if you miss the slightest trace of fungus, the trouble may start up again.

Prevention is better than cure. See that timber is kept dry; see that it is well ventilated and never, never block up air bricks 'to keep out the draughts'. That ventilation is your assurance against dry rot.

Wet rot: Another common trouble, wet rot is also caused by damp, but the moisture content has to be nearer 50 per cent. There are whitish strands, but damage is not so severe, and drying the wood immediately stops the trouble. So cure the damp as quickly as possible.

If you need advice on any aspect of timber trouble, contact the British Wood Preserving Association who know the firms who specialise in dealing with these problems. And, if you are having a house built, insist on treated timbers which have been pressure impregnated with preservatives. The troubles we have been discussing will then never be your worry.

FLOOR TILES

By far the easiest way of putting down sheet floor covering is to use tiles. They are easy to manage, easy to cut to fit awkward spots, and the pattern of your floor is almost infinitely variable. Tiles are available in many materials, including vinyl, plastic and cork. And if you want a natural timber finish, there are parquet tiles in a number of patterns and thicknesses.

Methods of laying have undergone a revolution; the old system of spreading adhesive on the floor and pressing tiles on to it has almost disappeared. Instead, you can get self-adhesive tiles. However, by far the most important part of floor tiling is preparation of the surface. The floor must be clean, dry and smooth. Let's look at each of those points.

The floor must be clean because no adhesive will stick to dust, dirt or grease. The floor must be dry because rising damp, perhaps coming up through a concrete floor, can ruin many floor tiles, or at least destroy the adhesive. The floor must be smooth because the tiles will, in a very short time, show up every irregularity, and in fact magnify the fault in the shiny surface. With a timber floor, be sure to remove all old floor covering nails and old line sprigs. If the boards are old and wavy, and if you can afford it, cover the floor with standard grade hardboard. This will provide an excellent surface for the tiles, and it will increase the life of the floorcovering many times over.

Just one important point if you plan to board over the floor. Consider whether you will ever need access to the space under the floor, either for electrical extensions, gas or water connections. If in doubt, a panel screwed down which can be raised without too much difficulty may well save you a lot of upheaval.

With a concrete floor, or an old quarry tiled or brick floor, you can get a smooth level surface by using a screeding compound. This is available from most builders' merchants.

When you have decided which tiles to use, get hold of the literature from the company concerned; this will give full

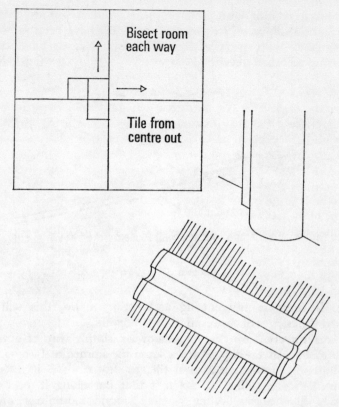

Setting out a room for tiling, and using a shape tracer for awkward trimming

details of their tiles. Most firms will also supply a squared chart which is very useful. On it you can mark your exact floor area, then you can colour in your pattern. By counting squares, you will then know just how many of each colour you need.

Most manufacturers also supply a leaflet giving full details on how to lay and cut the tiles, so we don't really need to go into a lot of detail here. So, having bought your tiles and prepared the floor surface, bisect the opposite walls of the room, chalk a piece of string, and snap a chalk line each way so that you divide the room into quarters. Start laying from the middle, where the lines cross, and tackle one quarter of the room at a

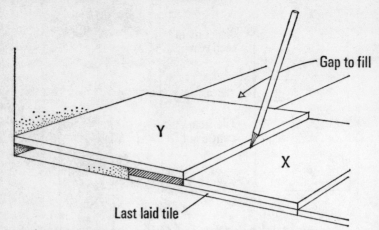

Tile Y rests on tile X and touches wall. Piece marked X, when cut, will fit gap.

How to cut a tile to fit a gap

time. If there is any cutting and fitting to do, this will be around the border of the room.

The illustration on this page shows a simple way of cutting a tile to fit a given gap. Place a loose tile immediately over the last laid one. Extend a second tile, as shown, until it rests on the wall. Score a line on the first tile; cut along it, and this tile will fit the gap. When cutting around mouldings, unless you have a proper template former, use a strip of cored solder shaped to fit the moulding, then transfer the shape to the tile. Incidentally, vinyl tiles cut much more easily if they are warmed first.

Another simple tip. If you do use tiles which require adhesive to be spread on the floor, be sure to clean any adhesive which gets on the face of the tiles as you go. Don't let it set, or it is practically impossible to remove. Also, keep a tile or two of each colour chosen in case of emergency. Tiles do get damaged, but it is not too difficult to get one up without disturbing the others. A hot iron applied over brown paper will make a tile easier to rip out, then you can clean off the adhesive using petrol or other solvent.

Finally, if using spirit-based adhesives, do read very carefully the directions on the can concerning ventilation and the elimina-

REPAIRS AND JOBS INSIDE THE HOUSE

tion of naked flames. A build up of fumes, plus an exposed flame, could be fatal.

PARQUET FLOORING

Like many other decorative jobs about the house, parquet laying used to be looked upon as strictly for the tradesman. Today, parquet panels are available which are as easy to lay as tiles, and you can get a really superb result at the first attempt.

But before looking at the panels, just a word about the floor. It is essential – as when laying vinyl tiles – that it is carefully prepared. It must be free from nails, tacks and other obstructions. Proud knots should be planed down and loose boards screwed or nailed in place. If the floor is dirty use the minimum of water to clean it, and allow it time to dry out. If a board floor is very uneven, put down standard grade hardboard, then lay your parquet on this.

With the floor prepared, what choice of material have you? There are many types available, but there are two basic methods of application which just about sums up the lot.

First, there is the permanent, thin parquet tile such as R.E. Ingham's Point One. As the name implies, the tile is 0.1 in. thick, but this is adequate to give many years of hard wear. In oak or mahogany, the tiles come ready treated with adhesive and protected by a plastic sheeting. They are supplied ready sanded and polished, and all you need is sufficient extra adhesive to spread on the floor.

Calculating quantity is easy, for the manufacturers supply a leaflet with a squared area on which you can mark out your room shape, then work out just what you need. When laying, adhesive is spread on the floor, allowed to become touch-dry, then the protective sheet is pulled from a tile, and the tile is laid. Bonding is immediate, and the tiles cannot be slid into place.

The second type of parquet is J. A. Hewetson's Lynx type panel, designed to produce a floating floor. These panels are thicker – about $\frac{1}{2}$ in. – and they are very accurately tongued and grooved. The panels are merely butted together, then tapped until they close up tight. They interlock on all sides, so they cannot work loose or ride up. No gluing or pinning is necessary, and the panels are supplied ready sanded and sealed and polished.

One advantage of this system is that the floor covering is not a fixture. If you wish, you can lift the panels and take them with you if you move. And, apart from use as a complete floorcovering, Lynx panels are very popular as surrounds for carpets, forming a well into which the carpet can be fitted.

Just a word of advice. Although parquet is pretty tough, it is a good idea to use rugs and runners to take the brunt of everyday traffic. Gritty shoes can make nasty scratches on the toughest of timber floors.

SOLID FLOORS

Solid floors present their own problems – probably the biggest is that of uneven surfaces. While you may disguise unevenness under a thick carpet and underlay, you certainly won't under modern thin floor coverings such as vinyl. However, treatment of an uneven solid floor has been greatly simplified with the introduction of screeding compounds. These are very easy to lay, and a very smooth finish – thanks to the self-levelling nature of the screed. Such a screed can be feathered right down to nothing, so you have no problem with raising skirting boards and cutting bits off door bases. Old quarry tiles, flagstones or bricks may be covered with a screeding compound too, giving you a brand new floor surface which will take any covering and show it off to best advantage.

Another common trouble with solid floors is damp, and folk have a job deciding the cause. The two main causes are condensation and rising damp, and it is not too difficult to tell one from the other. Condensation will form on the surface of impervious materials such as lino or vinyl at the same time as moisture condenses on windows.

If you lift the vinyl, the floor will be dry underneath. Beads of moisture can also form on quarry tiles in the same way, and you can cure the trouble merely by separating the cold floor surface from the floor covering. You can buy special cork underlays for hard floor coverings, or you can use thin expanded polystyrene – or buy one of the cushioned vinyl floor coverings which has a built-in underlay. With such insulation, you should get no more condensation, unless conditions are very severe.

Rising damp is more serious. You may find slight trouble when you lift vinyl sheeting and find damp areas under it. Damp under lino will be more quickly spotted, for the damp will ruin and warp the lino, making it cracked and brittle. In carpeted areas, you may get a musty smell and signs of mould growth.

A simple way of checking a solid floor is to get a piece of glass about 3 in. square, then build up a low wall of putty on the floor in the form of a 3 in. box. Press the glass on to this bed so that you leave a sealed gap under the glass, isolated by the putty from the room. If there is damp rising, you will soon see beads of moisture condensing on the underside of the glass.

With very slight damp, this moisture would normally have evaporated into the air until you cover the floor with an impervious layer, be it that small piece of glass or a complete layer of vinyl. Such damp is usually encountered in older properties where no effective damp-proof membrane was included in the floor, but it can appear in newer properties if the damp-proof barrier was damaged during laying.

Thanks to modern materials, you can deal with normal rising damp by sealing off the floor with special liquids such as Structoplast. Once treated, the floor may be covered again, but even so, take precautions to make sure there was no condensation either.

In a few rare cases, what is called hydrostatic pressure is encountered. This is usually where a house is built in a hollow or on the side of a hill where water under pressure may force its way up through a floor. So, if you are in such a location, and damp is persistent, call in your borough surveyor for advice. You cannot deal with this one yourself.

TIMBER FLOORS

Of all the house decoration, floors take the greatest punishment, especially with children around. So before renewing a floor covering, it is worth having a look at the floor to see that it is in good condition.

If a covering such as vinyl is to look its best and wear well, the floor must be really smooth. If you look carefully at older boarded floors, and perhaps put a steel rule on the floor and a light behind it, you will see how uneven the boards are. If this is the case, modern flooring materials will quickly conform to the irregular surface, and the result looks awful.

If boards are really bad, it may pay you to lift them and turn them over to present the unworn face, but you will appreciate this is a big job, and flooring nails are often difficult to pull. If you don't fancy this job, covering the boards with standard hardboard is a good alternative. Be sure to condition the boards before laying. This involves damping the rough side and stacking boards back to back for a couple of days in the room in which they will be laid. The boards will then adjust to the moisture content of the room, and you will get no trouble with buckling. Before laying, consider if you need any inspection panels to get at wiring or pipes. Then fix down your boards to the well-swept floor. If the floor is free from springing, deep drive panel pins are adequate, but if you can feel considerable spring in the floor, use serrated ring nails which won't pull out.

The board can now be covered with tiles or sheet material, underlay and carpet – or if you are tight for cash at the time, you can seal the hardboard with Ronseal or Bourne Seal to give an attractive, warm floor covering. If you plan to use your

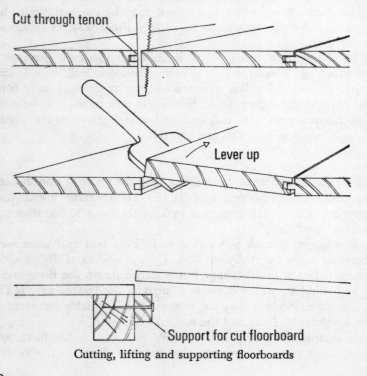

Cutting, lifting and supporting floorboards

hardboard as a floor covering for some time, choose oil-tempered board instead of standard. It looks better and it wears better.

If you inherit a hardwood floor that has been neglected, you can usually clean it up with fine wire wool dipped in turps. Always work with the wood grain to avoid scratching, then wipe off with clean rag. But if the blocks or strips are badly marked, you can probably improve the floor considerably by hiring a floor sanding machine for the day and giving it a good smoothing over.

The same machine can be used to take the humps off softwood flooring too, but if you decide to do this, spend time hunting for nails and tacks, and flooring nails proud of the surface. Any of these could ruin a sanding belt very quickly. If you encounter lots of small pins which are difficult to see, an old nylon stocking over your hand will soon snag on those you've missed.

Large gaps between floorboards can be sealed with papier mâché. It is far cheaper than proprietary fillers. Shred old newspapers and soak the shreds in water. Squeeze the water out, then add a fairly strong solution of glue size (of the type used to size walls). Work to a putty-like consistency and press into holes with an old kitchen knife or putty knife. If you want it to match for colour, you can add water stain as necessary. When dry, smooth off with glasspaper.

Larger gaps are best sealed with battens shaped to form a shallow wedge, glued and tapped home. When set, plane flush with the floor.

GAPS AND CRACKS

Most construction materials move in one way or another – either individually or one in relation to another. Hence the gaps and cracks we have to fill about the house. Let's look at a few useful materials.

Small cracks in wood frames about to be painted can be filled with putty after the wood has been primed, but if the actual wood is to be visible, or if there is the slightest chance of movement, use a coloured wood stopping to match the wood. There are interior and waterproof grades – make sure you choose the right one. In the main, cellulose fillers are not much good for wood.

Open-grain oak, such as you meet on some window sills, is very difficult to fill. Decorating shops and paint shops often stock gold size and whiting. This is a gooey mix which gets right into the wood pores. Ordinary water-bound fillers are pretty poor on this sort of job, for moisture gets trapped in air spaces, and as soon as the sun comes out, it is liable to expand the moisture in the cracks and push the paint off. If you must use ordinary wood primer, thin it a little and work it well down into cracks.

Joints between timber and masonry should never be filled with a rigid filler. Use a flexible mastic such as Seelastik which sets only on the surface. This material maintains a seal even if there is slight movement. Cracks in asbestos or roofing felt are best sealed with a bituminous mastic applied by trowel. This again does not set really hard, and it stays flexible.

Cracks or gaps between sheet glass, glazing bars or, in fact, any rigid materials, can be sealed with Sylglas tape or cord. The tape is best for large areas, and the cord is ideal for stuffing into smaller gaps. It is sticky stuff to use, but it seals well. Use it also for gaps between soil pipe and lavatory pan if the seal breaks down. Tamp it well home.

Gaps between gas barrel male and female threads, or any similar joints, can be sealed by binding the threads with what is called ptfe tape instead of the old hemp and red lead. This is far cleaner to use, and more effective.

Cracks in plaster where there is no movement can be filled with a cellulose filler. Take it just proud of the surface and then glasspaper the surface flush. If cracks are large and extensive, proprietary fillers can prove expensive; switch to Keenes cement. This is available in 7 lb. bags at only a fraction of the cost. Only one word of warning; it goes off rather quickly, so don't mix more than you can use in about five minutes. An alternative with a longer setting time is Sirapite plaster.

For cracks between floorboards, use papier mâché, or wedge-shaped battens, as mentioned earlier.

STAIRS AND REPAIRS
There's nothing worse than the lovely soft tread of a nice stair carpet broken by the harsh squeak of faulty stairs. So if you are having the carpet up, or putting down a new one, spend ten minutes going up and down, applying weight in different spots

REPAIRS AND JOBS INSIDE THE HOUSE

to try to produce squeaks. Mark the spots.

Most squeaks originate from loose wedges on the underside of the staircase, so if you can get underneath the stairs, this will simplify the job. An understair cupboard is ideal. You will see that wedge-shaped pieces of wood have been forced between the upright part of the stair (riser) and the horizontal section (tread), holding them tight in a board (string) at each side. If the wedges shrink, or if glue fails, the wedges work loose and the stair parts can move.

Remove all loose wedges, clean off old glue, apply new wood glue and tap each wedge firmly back in place. Use the treads repaired as little as possible until the glue has set.

This job is more difficult in homes where there is no access underneath. In this case, you will have to try to bring offending pieces together by means of screws. Locate the source of a squeak as near as possible, then drill a hole the size of the screw shank in just the tread immediately above the riser it is resting on. Drill a smaller hole down into the edge of the riser, then drive home a wood screw until it pulls the two parts together. In most cases this will eliminate a squeak completely. A little talc or French chalk puffed into gaps acts as a lubricant which will kill any remaining tiny noises.

If you have central heating and don't use humidifiers, you may find that the treads and risers have shrunk slightly in the housings holding them. As you can't get at the wedges, drill a hole, steeply angled sideways, in the tread so that a screw can be driven through into the string (the strings are the stair supports). When pulled tight, this should prevent movement.

You may also find gaps where one string meets the wall, also due to shrinkage. It is best to fill such cracks with a mastic rather than normal filler or putty, as movement may continue, breaking the bond of any rigid filler. If decorating, you may be able to back this up by bringing about $\frac{1}{4}$ in. of paper on to the stair board, thus hiding the joint completely. Don't press the paper too tightly into the angle, or any tension may just rip the paper.

While working on the stairs, you may want to modernise the banister and rail in some way. Folk often merely block in with hardboard then paper to match the hall, and while this looks neat, it can tend to make the stairs very dark plus making them feel narrow, even if they are not.

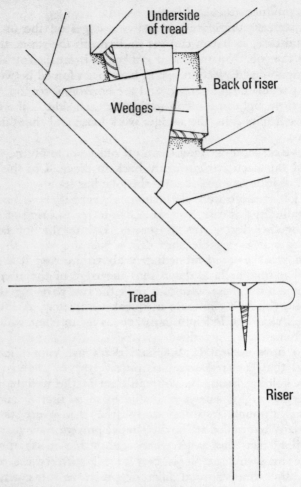

Wedging underneath and screwing down through stair treads to cure squeaks

Probably a better way is to remove some of the banister rails, leaving only those which are needed for structural support. It is most important not to weaken the support offered by the rail – especially if you have children or elderly people in the house who lean heavily against the rail or who may even fall against it.

REPAIRS AND JOBS INSIDE THE HOUSE

Having removed the rails, fill in with panels of translucent plastic closely resembling patterned glass. This material is lighter than glass, and it won't shatter if knocked against. It can be fixed in place with a neat timber beading with perhaps just a little mastic added to prevent vibration. You will get light through the sheets to illuminate the stairway.

Finally, if you are modernising, what about the horrible tongued and grooved boarding so beloved by builders for filling in under the stairs? The simplest treatment is to buy decorator's scrim used for bridging joints, and cover the boards with this, sticking it in place. Get it as flat as possible. Then line over this horizontally with lining paper, and follow with a good quality wallpaper hung in the normal manner. This will, in most cases, give a very good finish.

STAIR CARPETS

Having trouble putting down that new stair carpet? Well, here are a few carpet tips to help. Make sure you have good quality carpet felts, and that they turn over the stair nosings. If you tack them, be sure the tacks are well sunk in. A stair carpet should have at least a couple of feet extra on the end so that the length can be moved periodically. This will avoid undue wear on the treads – but it is a bit of a bind having to move it. The extra length can usually be folded under to form a double thickness, either at the top on the landing, or at the bottom in the hall.

The hardest part of laying stair carpet is turning a corner. Where does the spare bit go? Well, whatever you do, don't cut it or you can never move the carpet. The simplest way is to make a vee-fold and lose the extra against an appropriate riser. If you don't mind cutting a riser, you can make a $\frac{1}{2}$ in. wide slot horizontally and tuck the spare material in. This is more difficult, but it does avoid a bulge.

If you have a modern open-plan staircase, you won't want a full-length stair carpet anyway. Stair pads are the answer, but they will need holding in place. There are two ways; Velcro tape or special heavy-duty press studs. With the studs, the stud piece has a slot in the dome to allow you to screw the dome to the tread. Then the press stud part is sewn to the underside of the carpet. At least four press studs will be needed for each pad. Be sure to drill start holes in the tread first.

If you are not keen on drilling holes in your woodwork, then use Velcro tape. This is the tape that has two parts; one with minute loops and the other with tiny hooks. Press the two parts together, and they grip firmly.

Glue small strips to the tread with contact adhesive, then stick the mating parts to the underside of the carpet making sure they are in the right place to match up. You will find the carpet pads will be held firmly, yet can be pulled away when required.

Leaving the stairs, you might find that hall carpet runners often tend to slide about. If this happens to you, make use of Velcro strips here, too. They will hold the runner firmly in in place. The press studs can also be used if you don't mind boring holes in your floor. There is a third alternative. You can buy a special rubberised netting which can be laid under the runner. It doesn't need any fixing, but it will effectively prevent the carpet from moving.

Another trouble that arises with runners and stair pads is that of frayed edges. Carpets with a dimpled underlay already bonded on do not fray, but unbacked carpets can, if not sealed. You can buy special carpet binding tapes in a number of colours and with a powerful adhesive backing protected by a ribbed plastic strip. The adhesive is pressure-sensitive and grips very firmly.

Alternatively, you can buy a special latex carpet backing liquid which can be painted on the raw edges. Whitish in colour, the latex dries almost clear and it effectively binds together the backing. Once set, you can give a final trim to the edge with no fear of further fraying.

CURTAIN RAILS

One job that looks as if it should be easy – but often turns out to be tough – is fixing a curtain rail. If you inherit a house with battens already fixed to the wall, there is no difficulty, but if you have to fix direct to the wall, there could be trouble.

Above most windows, and in particular above large picture windows, there is a pretty hefty reinforced concrete lintel. This will have been covered with plaster, and there it hides – until you try to get a drill into it! You can blunt many a masonry drill on this stuff, and it is very unwise to resort to jumping tool and hammer as the vibration so often loosens the plaster. So what to do?

The simplest way today is to use a power tool with hammer action – a number of modern D.I.Y. drills have the action as an optional extra. By moving a switch, an impacting action is added which makes reinforced concrete easy meat. Even so, take it easy and don't apply too much force, or you will damage the hardened masonry drill tip.

If you don't want to use this method, an alternative is to drill a few small holes, designed to locate the extremities of the lintel. Then put up a batten wider than the lintel and put your main support screws into brick. You can drill a hole centrally at plaster depth just to keep the batten from sagging and this will be adequate for lightweight curtains. But if you have heavy ones, give extra support by using contact adhesive. Apply the adhesive to bare plaster and to the rear of the batten, and allow both surfaces to become touch dry. Then carefully locate your batten and see that the outer screws find holes, then press the batten home. A tap with a rubber mallet will give a firm bond.

Another way of avoiding the lintel is to fix above it – assuming the window does not go up to ceiling height! This will mean that your curtains will need to be longer, but the overall effect can be good, as it tends to make the window look larger than it really is.

Yet another method is to fix your rail direct to the ceiling instead of to the wall. You will see that most rails have holes for overhead fixing and, again, floor to ceiling curtains can look most effective, adding a completely new dimension to a room. If you do this you must locate the joists above the screw into this. Just hope that they are at right angles to your rail! If not, you may have to fix boards in the loft between the joists so that you can screw into the boards. Small support blocks holding the boards to the joists will take the strain off the ceiling plaster. Finally, screw the blocks in place – don't nail them. The vibration of nailing can cause damage to ceiling plaster. And do make sure that the screws that you use to fix your new rail to the batten do not go through to the wall. Pressure could push the batten from the wall.

Very often, users of even modern rails find the runners tend to judder and prove difficult to move. Lubrication is all that is needed. Use silicone lubricant (available in aerosols), but get the curtains out of the way first! This lubricant dries in a few minutes, leaving behind enough silicone to make sliding easy. If you haven't got an aerosol, use a little silicone wax polish on a duster. Repeat the treatment when the wax wears off. Don't use oil; makes a mess and some plastics are affected by it.

Do not confine your curtain-rail-fixing activities to new situations. Why not turf out old rails as you decorate room by room? It really is incredible how many folk will completely transform a room – and still leave up the old brass rail and roller wheels that went in when the house was built. Scrap the lot – and buy new rail which is both efficient and attractive to look at.

PLUGGING AND FIXING THINGS TO WALLS

When plugging walls, the simplest tool for making the holes is the jumping tool which is used in conjunction with a hammer. Smart taps drive the hardened tip of the tool into the wall, and slow rotation of the tool gives a clean hole. For large holes you can get star drills which are used in the same way.

However, while ideal for plain walls, on plastered surfaces the vibration can loosen the plaster, so here it is far better to use a tungsten carbide tipped masonry drill in either a hand drill or a power drill. If you use a power drill, use, if possible, one with speed reduction, using the slowest speed. Keep the tipped drill under pressure for a few seconds, then ease off to let the tip clear. Never let the tip just whistle round. You will merely blunt the cutting edges.

For solid walls, there are two basic ways of plugging prior to putting in a screw. First, there is the common wall plug, available either in fibre or plastic. For the best results, the drill, screw and plug should all be of corresponding sizes. The length of the plug should equal the thread length of the screw. Make sure that your hole is deep enough to take the screw – or you will pull the plug out of the wall. Secondly, there is the fibre plugging compound which is damped with a little water, kneaded until pliable, then tamped into the hole. The advantage of this method is that the compound will fill an irregular or oversize hole, where it hardens off after the screw has been driven home.

What of walls of hollow construction? Both methods mentioned are out if the hole must go through to the cavity. Instead you need one of the special devices produced for just this.

A spring toggle is ideal for fixing to hollow ceilings, but it can also be used on walls of thin section. The wings of the device are closed under spring tension, pushed through the hole and they will open out when they get right through. This device cannot be withdrawn, so make sure the item to be fixed is put on the screw before inserting the wings. (see page 41).

A gravity toggle is designed for thin partitions. The item to be fixed is threaded on the screw, the toggle is fed through the hole and, once through, the hinged section drops forming an anchorage.

A wall anchor is for walls of fairly thin section; this device has the advantage that, once fixed, the screw can be withdrawn, leaving the anchor in place. So the item to be fixed needn't be threaded on first. The anchor is pushed into the hole, then as the screw is turned, the soft metal wings are forced up the thread until they contact the rear face of the wall.

Then there is a little device which consists of a rubber sleeve with a threaded metal insert in one end. As the screw is turned, the sleeve is pulled up, spreading the rubber and making it grip firmly in any hole. If the material is very thin, the nut will bulge out on the far side, giving a firm vibration-free fixing. The nut can be loosened and withdrawn any time. And even this is not really the end of the list, for there are heavy-duty toggles and a whole range of expansion bolts for really tough fixing jobs.

For many jobs, too, like fixing battens to walls, you can simply use masonry nails, designed to be driven straight into the brickwork, rather than plugs. Be sure that you get the right length of nails for the job in hand. These nails must not be too long, or they will split the bricks. Note that, if your wall is made of lightweight building blocks, more likely than not you can nail or screw straight into the material without any trouble.

MAKING A HATCHWAY

A hatch between kitchen and dining room can be a real boon, especially where a family is concerned. If your home hasn't one, think about putting one in next time you decorate.

The first consideration is size. If you don't go wider than

about 2 ft. the brickwork above your hole in the wall needs no support. But if you plan to go bigger, you really need a length of heavy angle iron to set in the wall either side to take the weight. If you go wider than the 2 ft. mentioned, the angle iron can be let into the mortar joints before removing brickwork below. If you want to go really wide to make a feature opening, then ask the advice of your borough surveyor. You may need a lintel if the wall above is load-bearing, and this can be tricky.

Let us, however, assume that you settle for a hole 2 ft wide. First mark out the area in the kitchen on the plaster. Then get a long masonry drill of any size that's not too big and drill a hole right through the wall at each corner. You can now see in the dining room where the hole will be. Now, with a steel chisel and club hammer, tap a line through the wall plaster right round the rectangle, through to the bricks or breeze blocks. Then ease away chunks of plaster to reveal the wall.

Carefully chip away at the mortar between the bricks. Try not to go right through to the plaster on the other side, then you will keep most of the mess on one side of the wall.

After a while you should be able to ease out bricks by levering and wiggling until you are left with only whole bricks which bridge the line of the hatch. These will have to be cut through with taps on a sharp bolster (a wide blade chisel).

Clean out all debris, then go round to the other side. Now if your plaster is still sound, get an old hacksaw blade and grip it in some form of handle. Enlarge one of the holes through the plaster, saw through it, working all round the hole. It may sound daft, but it works provided the bond between plaster and brick is good. If it isn't you will have to resort to chisel and hammer.

With the hole complete, you now need a timber frame. Make this like an open box, dead square; a shade smaller than the hole, and deeper than the thickness of the wall. If you have room, make it at least two or three inches wider. Wedge the frame squarely in place with wood wedges, and secure it by means of wall plugs and screws.

Fill the gaps around the frame with filler – Keenes cement is cheap and quick setting – and smooth the filler dead level with the wall plaster, or you will see any irregularities when you hang wallpaper. Rub smooth when set, then rub down your new woodwork.

How you finish off is up to you. You can have a flap which lets down to form a platform. Or you can fix doors which open out.

FLUE TROUBLES

It seems these days that you no sooner solve one problem in the home when you create another. A modern boiler is far more efficient in all respects than its counterpart of a few years ago. In consequence, heat produced is accurately controlled and well distributed, and less heated air goes up the flue. This in turn means that the interior of the flue is far cooler, and instead of gases passing out, they often condense on the flue lining.

These condensed fluids are highly corrosive, and they very soon attack the flue lining, seeping through the chimney fabric and appearing as stains on inside walls and chimney breasts. If trouble goes unchecked, the mortar in the chimney may be damaged and, as it disintegrates, the chimney may become distorted to such an extent that a really severe wind brings it down. Housewives inadvertently increase the damage by burning damp rubbish and wet fuel on the boiler, producing even more moisture to be condensed.

The only sure way of preventing this trouble if you have a high efficiency boiler – and certainly if you install a new gas-fired boiler – is to line the flue.

The old method used to be to build up an interior lining of salt-glazed pipes, as used for drain work, but the modern equivalent is the flexible stainless steel flue lining. This is fed down the old flue, secured to the boiler flue pipe and the top of the flue, so that gases are completely separated from the walls of the old flue. You should check with the builders' merchant whether you should use aluminium or stainless steel.

There is another alternative, but you don't do this yourself – it is done for you by Rentokil. In this system, an inflated 'sausage' is inserted in the flue for its full height. Then, while held there, a lightweight material is poured around it, where it quickly sets. The sausage is then removed, leaving a new flue passage surrounded by insulation which again keeps gases from the old flue.

Finally, what about stained plaster and decorations? Damaged plaster will of course have to be replaced, but where only staining has taken place, provided that the source of the trouble has been eliminated, you can seal off the stain with a good aluminium primer applied to the plaster. Don't use aluminium paint; the special primer has a scale-like structure to make a good seal.

An alternative is to use one of the damp-resisting foils sold by builders' merchants for treating damp walls. We are not keen on them for damp walls as they only hide the trouble, but for sealing off stains they are ideal. Then, after one of these methods has been applied, the wall can be redecorated.

If you should decide to line the flue yourself, check first that the stack is in good shape and not distorted. And if you do climb up to it, be sure to use scaffolding or a proper roof ladder. A chimney stack is a very heavy item to topple through your roof!

BLOCKING OFF A FIREPLACE

With central heating becoming more and more commonplace, the old open fireplace is now obsolete in many homes. This particularly applies to the monstrosities with cast iron surrounds which used to be so popular in bedrooms. So it is not surprising that many folk want to take out the old fireplace and fill the gap. The space can then be used more profitably for furniture – or you can fit a modern panel fire.

One point you should bear in mind before starting work is that an open fireplace affords good room ventilation. If you block off the flue, fit a ventilator, or you may well get trouble through lack of air movement.

How does one get out the old fireplace? If you look carefully either side of the surround – probably buried under wallpaper – you will find a couple of lugs held with screws. These hold the fireplace surround in contact with the wall. Unscrew the screws or cut through the lugs with a cold chisel. You would do well to have some help available when doing this job, for many fire surrounds are deceptively heavy. This applies particularly with tiled surrounds.

With the surround out, you will have quite a bit of mess to clean up. It is then a matter of deciding how you want to block in the hole. You can insert a piece of board, such as asbestos fibre board, in the hole so that it lies flush with the surface. It can then be plastered in to give a flush finish. Or you may choose to make a simple batten framework and cover

REPAIRS AND JOBS INSIDE THE HOUSE

this with asbestos fibre board. The ventilator may be a simple hit and miss type inserted either in the new board, or in the actual chimney breast.

Once the panel is in place, you can paint or paper over it. But if you plan to fit an electric panel fire, you would do well to get a fitting leaflet first so that you can tailor your frame to take the fire. This is not difficult, but it does involve having battens in the right place.

One other important point. If you block off an unwanted fireplace, it is wise to fit a half round tile or some form of capping pot to prevent rain getting into the chimney. When the flue was in use, this moisture would have evaporated, but if there is little or no air movement, the damp could cause the stack to deteriorate and cause staining in the house.

DIVIDING A ROOM

While large open plan areas in the home have their appeal, there are decided snags as the family grows up and there are varieties of activities to be pursued. Similarly, a spacious bedroom may be of far more value to the growing family if divided in two, providing an extra room.

Temporary divisions are not easy to come by, though you can buy concertina-style sliding partitions. The snag here is that such partitions are not soundproof, thereby rather defeating the object of the exercise. Similarly, making folding partitions is a possibility, but the sturdy construction required adds problems.

Probably the best way of dividing is to make a permanent alteration. It pays to sit down and plan on paper just how the job can be tackled. This is particularly important with bedrooms, for if possible you should make the division so that there is a door for each room so you don't have to pass from one room into the other. And, if possible, arrange a window for each room – although this cannot always be done.

Don't be afraid of making one room on the small side. With careful planning, the smaller room can take a single bed and fitted furniture – ample for a child of any age.

If your partition is on a solid ground floor, you can work with lightweight building blocks, which are easy to erect, light to handle, and have good sound insulation. Sheet plasterboard may then be stuck to either side, providing a good surface for decorating. Alternatively, you can build with timber, say 3 in. by 2 in, rough sawn, and make a very simple framework over which plasterboard can be nailed. This method can be used on a timber floor too.

A good alternative for any floor is to use one of the proprietary panelling systems. Take a tip, though; order fairly narrow panels if you have to get them upstairs! A panel 8 ft. 6 in. high and 3 ft. wide, with nothing to get hold of or grip can offer an intriguing problem when there are stairs to negotiate. The panels are lifted on to a timber sole plate, at the same time, locking the top of the panel around a batten fixed to the ceiling. Special vertical battens are used to join one panel to the next, and after adding a skirting board, the whole structure is extremely strong and not too bad as far as soundproofing is concerned. A special tape and joint filler is available to cover joints to give a completely unbroken surface. This is probably the most tricky operation, but it is not too difficult.

A point to bear in mind is wiring. You may wish to add an extra electric socket outlet in your newly constructed room, in which case you may be able to feed your cable along within the new wall. You may also have to alter the positions of wall light switches – and add a new one – and alter the position of ceiling pendants. This is work to be tackled before you re-decorate.

UP ALOFT

With space at a premium in our homes, it is a great pity that the majority of houses are still built with no regard whatsoever for use of loft space. Yet that space can make a tremendous difference to any growing family. In fact, most modern homes have timbers of such small section in the loft 'to keep the price down', that you would be chancing your arm to put even a trunk up there!

Assuming your loft is usable, at least it is worth exploiting as storage space – and that means you need to be able to get up and down easily. Loft ladders are available in a wide variety of types to suit all pockets.

The next important factor is good lighting. Don't use a length of trailing flex with swinging lampholder. Spend a bit of time wiring in a couple of points with a switch where it can be reached as you climb the ladder. One neat idea is to make a translucent hatch cover with strip lights inside. When shut, the hatch illuminates the upstairs landing. When swung up into the loft, in the open position, the cover illuminates the interior of the loft.

Flooring is the next consideration. Balancing from one joist to the next is a highly precarious way of getting about, and so often it ends with a foot through the ceiling! Boarding over is well worth while, but before you do that, put insulating material between the joists. This can be a glass fibre or a loose-fill material. Chipboard is a good material for a floor. You will of course have to choose sheet sizes by the hatch opening, but the pieces are easily secured with screws. Never use nails; you may spoil the ceilings below by vibration, and if you have the slightest doubt about the strength of the joists, contact your local borough surveyor and ask his advice.

If your roof is felted, no dirt will be able to blow into the roof space, but if your house is an older one and you can see daylight between the tiles, some sealing off is advisable. You can do this by stapling a reflective foil building paper to the rafters, or by nailing plasterboard or weather-resistant fibreboard to the rafters. Some folk frown on this and say you are encouraging rot, but in our experience this is not true, for there is adequate ventilation around the now hidden joists due to gaps between tiles.

If your family is outgrowing your cherished home, you may have living space up aloft. Maybe a fair size bedroom, plus a jolly good den for the boys – and their train set. Contact the building inspector of your local authority on this one and have a chat about it. True, you must conform with certain Building Regulations with regard to strength and headroom. You may have to spend money on joist strengthening and the moving of certain timbers, but if you weigh this against the cost of moving to a larger home, it may be well worth the money.

Also consider the introduction of dormer windows which let in daylight. You may even have room to pinch a part of one room to put in a proper staircase, because, again, there are regulations you must meet with regard to access to living accommodation. Don't be too alarmed at this, for the larger joinery firms can supply prefabricated staircases, or they can tailor-make a staircase to fit your particular needs.

CHAPTER FIVE
Decorating

PAINTING TIPS

Please don't turn paint cans upside down to prevent paint skinning. It doesn't! You merely end up with a skin at the bottom instead of the top. It is better to lay a circle of aluminium foil on top of the paint; better still, move the paint to a smaller, airtight container.

Don't use new paint brushes for top coat. Dust and bristles will ruin the finish. Use them on undercoat until well worn in and then use them for finishing work. And clean up spots and splashes as you go, using brush cleaner. Once paint has dried it takes much hard work to move.

Take paint on window frames $\frac{1}{8}$ in. on to the glass to seal the gap between putty and glass. If you don't, moisture will get under your paint and push it off.

Use a paint kettle (which holds $1\frac{1}{2}$–2 pints) which makes the job easier and saves wasting paint, and save on cleaning your paint kettle by lining it with household foil or plastic. When you finish painting, remove the foil and your kettle is ready for immediate re-use.

If you intend painting large areas such as walls – or door panels – a paint roller or pad brush is ideal. You will find there are three main types of roller. The mohair, short pile, roller is best suited for gloss paints and really fine finishes. And it needs careful cleaning. Pad brushes are also mohair. The lambswool roller is ideal for textured surfaces, as the deep pile gets into crevices. It is best used with emulsion paint. The foam plastic roller is suitable for general painting on reasonably smooth surfaces, but it does tend to spatter easily, and you must learn not to apply any pressure or you will squeeze paint out of the roller. Always work in all directions with a roller or pad brush – not as you would with a paint brush.

DECORATING

To clean a brush without messing your hands, put a little brush cleaner in an undamaged polythene bag. Pop in the brush bristles and work in the cleaner from outside. Don't leave paint brushes for long periods in water; the ferrules will rust. If you must leave brushes for a while, better to charge them with paint, then wrap them in foil to exclude all air. For really long periods, clean them properly.

A nylon stocking fixed over a paint tin will strain out skin and bits. Be sure the stocking is a recently washed one or it may be harbouring dust. Or you can buy proper strainers. Be sure to stir all paints thoroughly before using. Failure to do so is one cause of poor drying and poor covering power.

REMOVING A PICTURE RAIL

To remove a picture rail, take it easy, or you may have a lot of plastering to do. Use a block of wood as a fulcrum, and an old chisel as a lever, and see if the rail will give. If the nails holding it are not too tightly home, they may pull away, and the job will be simple.

But if you meet cut nails which have rusted in the plaster, use a tenon or sheet saw to cut through the rail as near to the nails as possible. Then break the wood away from the nails.

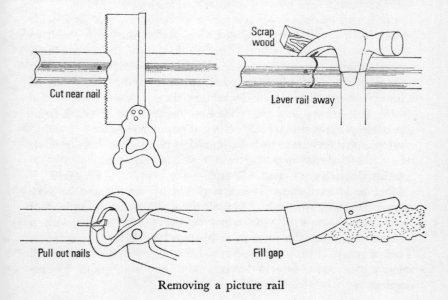

Removing a picture rail

You can then wiggle the nails out at leisure with pincers.

You will probably find that as the rail was put up prior to final plastering, the plaster above and below the rail are on slightly different levels. There is little you can do about this except make as neat a joint between the two as you can. Don't use a proprietary cellulose filler here, as it will work out rather expensive. Use Keenes cement, which is much cheaper, and easy to smooth when dry. Take the cement a little proud of the surface, then use the edge of a cabinet scraper to bring it level with the existing plaster.

PREPARATION

However large or small the job you plan to tackle, the finished result will depend so much on preparation. This is of course the worst part of the project, and for that reason it is often skimped.

Examine the room you are to work in. If there are signs of damp, locate the cause and get things put right before you start or you will be wasting your time and money. Treat walls attacked by mildew and fungus with a fungicidal wash to kill off all spores. Seal stain marks with aluminium primer, or the stain will come through your new decoration. Remove damaged areas of plaster and fill with plaster or Keenes cement.

Look, too, for signs of dry rot or woodworm, and deal with these. And if you need new electrical socket outlets or wish to wire for wall lights, now is the time to do the plaster channelling.

Let us assume that the whole room is to be redecorated. The ceiling is the best place to start – after clearing the room of course, and putting down decorating sheets. Always tackle the ceiling before stripping the walls because splashes of muck from the ceiling will come off with the wallpaper later on.

If you are fortunate to have emulsion painted ceilings, a wash down with sugar soap and water will clean it sufficiently to repaint. If yours is a water-bound distempered ceiling, get it all off before redecorating. This is a rotten job and it can be very messy. The way we do it is to soak the ceiling with a lambswool roller, then scrape off the worst of the ceiling white with a scraper, collecting the mess in a dustpan held below the scraper. Then a rough cloth – such as an old towel – soaked in water will remove the remaining distemper. Use emulsion paint for re-decorating.

If your ceiling white is old and hard, rather than trying to scrape it off, seal it with a special liquid called Kinseal then paint over it with emulsion paint. If the ceiling has been lined, then distempered, and the distemper is loose, the best thing to do is soften the lot and pull the paper away and start again.

With your ceiling clean, repaint it before wall stripping – unless wallpaper and paint meet in the corner. If they do, it is best to strip the paper away from the corner so that you can carry paint just on to the wall. Then, when you paper, should you cut a length a shade short, you will not have a noticeable gap between paint and paper.

By the way, if you choose to use expanded polystyrene ceiling tiles, use non-flam grade in the kitchen at least. Pans on fire have often set fire to ceiling tiles, thus doing more damage than would otherwise have occurred. And nowadays, the old blob method of applying adhesive is no longer approved. Use the all-over method.

Next strip off the wallpaper. Never paper over old paper. It is a bad habit, and it is often disappointing as the new paper can loosen or blister the old stuff. Also stains and marks have a habit of working through in time. Most papers come off with adequate soaking, but if they are of the washable or wipable variety, you may have to score the surface to allow the water in. A Cintride abrasive disc is useful for this, but don't be too rough.

To hold water in contact with a heavyweight paper, it is a good idea to add a little cellulose paste to the water plus a few spots of liquid detergent. But if you really have trouble, try to hire a steam wallpaper stripper for a day. These are usually propane gas fired and the steam produced is applied to the wall by means of a flat plate. The steam quickly loosens the toughest of papers.

With all the paper off, allow the walls to dry, then go over with glasspaper to remove all nibs and projections. You can feel rough spots with your hand. Then have a really good clean up to remove all damp paper. If it dries on skirtings or picture rails, it is hard to shift.

Now is the time to strip off old paint, either with a chemical stripper or a blowlamp or blowtorch, depending upon your ability. The chemical is far safer, but more expensive. However, if the paint is in good shape, it will need only a wash with sugar soap and a rub with a stripping block. The stripping block contains pumice, and this removes the sheen from the gloss, providing a better key for new paint. Be sure to rinse well with clean water afterwards.

Now have a good clean up once more. A tacky rag is ideal for removing any remaining dust and dirt. The order after this will be – repaint, then paper.

PAINTING WOODWORK

Before any new paint is applied, make sure all cracks and gaps are filled with cellulose filler or with stopping. If you use putty for filling, apply this after priming, otherwise the bare wood will take the oil out of the putty, and the putty may shrink and fall out later on. Any resinous knots must be sealed with patent knotting (a saturated solution of shellac in methylated spirit) prior to painting, or the resin may bleed through later on.

Never paint over rust. Always scrape away all loose rust first and get to the very edge of the rust, even if you have to scrape a lot of paint off to find it. Then treat the surface with a rust inhibitor to prevent any further action.

All bare wood should be primed. The primer seals the pores of the wood, and provides a key for the undercoat which follows. It is the undercoat which provides body and obliterating power, and if one coat of undercoat does not obliterate an undercolour, apply a second coat. The top coat will add the sheen, but it has very little obliterating power. If you choose a one-coat paint, then you can dispense with undercoat. But you may need two top coats to obliterate another colour.

WALLPAPER HANGING

Before actually buying the wallcovering, remember that a random pattern needs little or no matching. So if this is your first attempt, this will give you a chance to practice getting the paper on without worrying about moving it up and down. And if the room has walls with corners not too true, avoid those beautiful Regency stripes! They will accentuate every error in the wall surface.

Plan to butt all your joints – but even so, if a wall is a little irregular, you may get a slight overlap. To allow for this, aways paper from a window wall away from the window. Then, if there should be a slight overlap anywhere, no shadow will be cast along the paper edge.

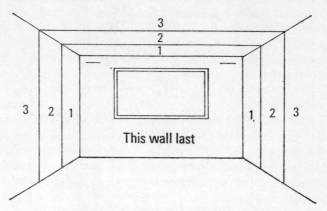

Order to tackle wall and ceiling covering

Always start the first length by dropping a plumb line to give you a true vertical. The edge of the window may not be, and if you start off wrong, you will be out all around the room. Somewhere you may have to lose your pattern matching (if there is one) and the place to do it is in a corner, preferably hidden from normal view.

If you are papering a chimney breast, it is a good idea, if you have a prominently patterned paper, to start from the middle of it in this case, so that your first length is half either side of the centre line. This gives a nice balanced appearance, and any mismatching can be lost in the chimney breast corners.

Very often the pattern repeat does not go exactly into the height to be papered, which can mean waste of paper. To avoid waste, it is often possible to work from alternate rolls of paper. If you really do run short, try to arrange so that patching is done at a point which will be covered by furniture. This sounds elementary, but it needs thinking about before you get into trouble.

Weight of paper is important too. The worst paper to hang is the very cheap, thin one which wrinkles and tears easily. It is not the ideal paper to learn with. A good medium weight paper is best – but do give it time to soak a little before hanging,

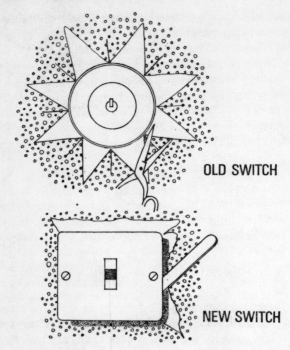

Trimming wall covering around light switches

or you may get bubbles which you cannot get rid of. The heavier the paper, the longer it needs to soak. Don't depend on bubbles drying out. In our experience, they rarely do.

Now for some of the difficulties encountered.

Blisters: There are usually two main causes here. The first – and most common – is not letting the paper soak long enough after pasting. This applies particularly to heavy papers, which should be pasted with a full-bodied paste, then left while one or two more pieces are pasted. The paper will then finish stretching before it is put on the wall. Second, papers can blister if placed over an impervious surface such as a painted wall subject to condensation. The damp soaks through the paper, cannot penetrate the wall, so it loosens the adhesive and expands the paper. One cure here is to line the wall with thin expanded polystyrene, then paper over this.

Lack of adhesion: Paper won't stick well to a distempered

wall. Very often the distemper breaks up and the paper comes away with it. You often see this where wall meets a ceiling and where distemper has been carried down on to the wall. Scrub the distemper off, however safe it may seem.

Paper doesn't stick well to a newly plastered wall either. Salts coming out of the plaster during natural drying can crystallise under the paper, then push it off. If you press loose patches you will hear a faint crunching noise. You can buy special paints to kill this efflorescence as it is called. Alternatively, leave the wall bare – or emulsion painted – until drying out has finished. Emulsion paint will still let the wall breathe.

Too weak a paste may also result in poor adhesion. If you choose a heavy paper such as one of the attractive Anaglypta patterns, use a full-bodied cold water paste, plus the old fashioned glue size on the wall, rather than a cellulose paste. You get better grip and certainly a stronger bond. Cellulose paste has a very high water content and therefore less solid matter. And this, after all, is the bit which counts in the end.

Mould: This is a common trouble in winter – and one which causes a lot of heartache. The nice new paper suddenly sprouts fine brown or purple dots which weren't on the pattern; or shows signs of another malady, which is a greenish fuzz. Unfortunately we know of no superficial treatment, as so often the mould is striking through from the wall below. It is a case of stripping off the paper, treating the wall with a fungicidal wash, then repapering, using a paste which contains a fungicide.

This also applies to vinyl wall coverings, where damp cannot dry out through the paper surface. You must use a special paste which contains a fungicide, or you will risk the growth of mould. Often, the mould is encouraged by cold wall surfaces with no flow of air over them – such as behind a piano or wardrobe. Warming the room and easing the furniture forward just a shade, may be enough to prevent the mould even starting to grow.

Dirty marks: If marks are superficial, such as mud or pencil, you may get them off with a rubber gum as used by artists on delicate papers. This crumbles up as it is used. Or pull the dough from the middle of a piece of bread; press it to form a lump of putty-like material, and rub with this. You can buy a proprietary product of similar consistency.

Grease marks: These are far more difficult to remove, as grease or fat on normal wallpaper soaks through and into the wall. We know of no effective way of drawing out the grease. You can deal with the trouble by scraping off the damaged area, treating the wall with carbon tetrachloride, then patching with a piece of matching paper by tearing the paper so that the edges are feathered under. In this way the paper can be made to go down flush, with no hard edges to catch the light. Of course, modern plastic coated papers or vinyls will not absorb grease.

Embossed papers: These are very popular but often they are spoiled by the pressing down of the mating edges so hard that the pattern is flattened. You don't notice anything until you stand back – then you see shiny vertical lines. Avoid this by pressing the paper down with a foam plastic paint roller or a soft pad of rag – not with the fingers.

Painting: Most papers can be emulsion painted provided that the surface is clean and grease-free. But there are exceptions. First, if the pattern is embossed so that you can see the old pattern through. Second, if there is a chance you may want to get the paper off in the near future. It makes the job far harder.

HIDING HUMPS AND BUMPS

In some homes, especially older ones, the plaster on internal walls is in pretty poor shape. And it can be a headache trying to hide the humps and bumps. So instead of worrying too much, why not try the opposite on feature walls and rough them up even more? If you can make a definite texture where at present there is just a mess, then so much the better.

One of the simplest ways of getting a texture is by using an Anaglypta paper. All good decorating shops should be able to show you a pattern book with these papers in, and you will see there is plenty of pattern variety – from plaster daub effects to attractive basket weave. They are easy to apply as long as you let them soak well, then use glue size on the wall and a nice full-bodied cold water paste. Once up, you can emulsion paint to taste – or you can buy a range with a white finish already applied.

True, the texture is mild, so if you want something more pronounced, look out for architectural panels. These are supplied by the panel, not by the roll, and they carry a very heavy relief. Again there are many patterns from random modernistic shapes, to really bold pebble designs. You need special adhesive for these panels, but application is not difficult.

Because of the high relief, the panels are best suited to smaller areas – but you certainly won't see any wall faults through!

Another relief material well tried over the years but still going strong is Lincrusta. You will find many decorating shops have a book of designs in this material. It closely resembles ordinary putty patterned on to a lining paper, and patterns vary from coils of rope to timber planks. You can get imitation timber panelling, too. Again, fixing is by special adhesive, and once in place the surface can be painted.

The latest material to join the textures is expanded polystyrene. Rolls of patterned plastic are also quite common. A new development is patterns and shapes cut from expanded polystyrene. The pieces are stuck on the wall, either at random or to a set repeating pattern, and by painting wall and plastic in contrasting colours or tones, some very interesting effects are possible. If you feel like a bit of fun, buy plastic sheeting as used for insulation, then buy a simple battery-operated hot wire cutter and cut your own shapes.

A rough plaster effect can look pleasing on a feature wall, and if you want to try your hand at this, do a bit of experimenting with Polyfilla. You may need quite a bit, and it has to go on the wall fairly thickly. First spread liberally with a trowel, then dab, smear and pull at it with a screwed up plastic bag or even a ball of newspaper. You can get some very interesting effects. The only difficulty is trying to remember how to repeat the effect over a whole wall! That's why it pays to be as random as possible. And keep the mix nice and dry or it will sag and go messy.

Painting these rough surfaces can be a bit tricky, but the best tool is a long hair lambswool roller or pad brush. Don't work too fast with the roller or you will throw paint all over the place.

Give a bit of thought to lighting. What you need is a light or lights as close to the wall surface as possible so that you throw shadows that really make the texture stand out. Wall lights are fine. A pendant in the middle of the room is useless.

CHAPTER SIX
Damp and its Cure

CONDENSATION

In a nutshell, condensation is what you get when warm, moisture-laden air comes into contact with a cold, dense surface. Warm air is able to hold far more water vapour than cold air, so when warm air is cooled, it releases moisture – which is deposited as drops of water. You will get condensation on absorbent surfaces too. But brickwork, plaster and wallpapers usually absorb the moisture, so no drops of water are seen.

The first essential when dealing with condensation is first to be quite sure that this is what your trouble is. You must be able to distinguish between damp caused by structural trouble, and deposited vapour. If damp patches appear on walls only on washing days, bath nights or when a lot of cooking is being done, the trouble is likely to be condensation. And this moisture will, almost without exception, appear on outside walls which, of course, are cold. Hardly ever do you find condensation appearing on internal dividing walls. Confirmation that the moisture is in fact condensation will be given by the windows being wet also.

If you find damp patches on external walls during very heavy rain, or patches of damp at skirting board level during damp weather, suspect structural damp caused by water finding its way into the house through the walls or through the damp-proof course. This sort of damp is a different matter altogether, and remedies for treating condensation will be useless in curing it.

Condensation trouble should be dealt with as soon as possible. It can ruin wallpaper by staining it or causing it to peel. It can also ruin paintwork, especially on window frames, and can make your house feel colder as well as giving it a musty smell.

An extractor fan is an ideal way of removing moisture-laden air from kitchen or bathroom. In the kitchen, a hood over the cooker and leading to the extractor fan can help in some cases, but in most homes the hood is dealing with only one source of steam, when in fact there are others – the kitchen sink, boiler and washing machine are likely culprits. A fan set high in the wall or window, without a hood, will deal with them all. The only snag, or course, is that in winter you are extracting warmth from your home, as well as damp air!

When painting walls in kitchen or bathroom, you can use what is called an anti-condensation paint. This acts as both an insulator (to stop the cold reaching the warm air inside the room) and an absorbent surface. This will eliminate streak marks on walls. On ceilings, expanded polystyrene tiles will act as an insulator; remember that if the loft is immediately above the ceiling, then loft insulation will help to prevent condensation, as well as saving money on fuel.

You may well argue that, as expanded polystyrene is such a good insulator, why not put it on walls, too? So you can; before wallpapering cold surfaces, cover them with thin sheet expanded polystyrene. You will probably find that at least two thicknesses are offered. The thicker the sheet, the better the insulation.

The material is stuck on with a special adhesive then the wallpaper is put on in the usual way with wallpaper adhesive. There is only one snag, and that is that the material is rather soft, so do use a heavy quality wallcovering, especially where furniture or children are likely to knock against it.

Double glazing of windows will cut out condensation there, provided that there is a good seal between the panes, but as a purely temporary measure, you can buy some special sponge strip which, when laid along the window sills, will absorb the moisture where it collects. The strip can be wrung out and replaced when it becomes saturated.

Warmth, surprisingly, can help to prevent condensation. The reason for is that, with continuous warmth, the walls absorb heat; with warm walls there is nowhere for the moisture-laden air to condense on. An electric tubular heater, placed at the base of a cold wall, is often sufficient to cure the trouble.

Oil heaters and badly flued gas fires, while being excellent sources of heat, produce water vapour in considerable quantities. So where there is condensation, this form of heating is likely to aggravate it. But a little thought will help to alleviate the trouble. In the kitchen, saucepan lids will reduce the amount of steam escaping into the atmosphere. In the bathroom, run a little cold water into the bath first then lead the hot into this by means of a length of hosepipe. Close doors leading from steam-laden rooms and so prevent the warm, moist air from reaching the colder parts of the house.

STRUCTURAL DAMP

Compared with condensation, structural damp is much more serious. So let us look at some of the troubles you may meet, beginning at the top of the house.

Damaged flashings: The joint which seals the gap between chimney and roof is called a flashing. If this is damaged or displaced, rain will seep down the stack and, possibly, through a bedroom ceiling. This is one of the jobs where it might be advisable to call in an expert, as the chimney is well out of reach of normal ladders. If you do it yourself, use Nuralite flashing; it is easier to manipulate than lead.

Displaced or damaged tiles: Again, damp patches on bedroom ceilings may point to this fault. Try to look for the source of the trouble in wet weather. Water may seep along a rafter for a long way before dripping down. If you can reach, you may be able to push the tile back in position. If the tile is cracked, a bituminous mastic compound will seal it until the tile can be replaced. If you get damp ceilings during snowy weather, it probably means that you live in a house with no felt under the tiles and snow is merely blowing in and melting.

A bitumen-impregnated building paper pinned to the rafters, and the ends led down and out at the eaves, will stop this. The end must go out of the roof so that any water collected does not stay in the loft.

Faulty gutters and down-pipes: These are frequently the cause of dampness. Check for rusted sections, open joints between sections, down-pipes blocked by nest or leaves, sagging gutters – or even non-existent gutters! So often, in heavy rain, water is allowed to pass into brickwork where it often finds a way on to an internal wall. Bituminous mastic, plastic metal, Sylglas tape and cord – or a thorough overhaul if necessary – will prevent further seepage.

Porous brickwork: There are many excellent damp-repelling

DAMP AND ITS CURE

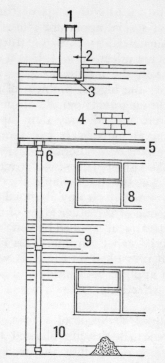

Ten danger points for damp. 1. Rain down unused chimneys. 2. Damaged pointing. 3. Damaged flashing. 4. Missing or cracked slates/tiles. 5. Faulty guttering. 6. Blocked downpipes. 7. Gaps around frames. 8. Missing putty. 9. Porous brickwork. 10. Missing, damaged or bridged damp-proof course

liquids available now which will effectively seal walls while still allowing them to breathe. Alternatively, you can use stone paint, cement paint or, for a decorative finish, a good quality exterior grade emulsion paint.

While you are at it, check the pointing, too. If this is in poor shape, damp will seep in. True, if you have cavity walls, the damp should not be able to bridge the gap, but so very often it seems that a wall tie (those metal pieces which tie together the two leaves of a cavity wall) is bridged by mortar droppings, and damp passes from one leaf to the other.

Gaps around frames: In time, timber frames shrink away from surrounding brickwork, leaving a gap into which rain can seep.

Such gaps should be sealed with a mastic compound such as is available in tubes or special applicator guns. This material seals the gap but remains flexible; thus any further movement in wall or timber does not affect the seal. If you should use cement, it is likely that in a very short time, the gap will reappear.

Rising damp: Here's the biggest problem of all. A damp-proof course that has disintegrated; no damp-proof course at all, or one that has been bridged, may show up as damp patches at skirting board level indoors. It can soon cause rotting of timbers as well as ruining decorations.

Damaged or non-existent damp-proof courses call for a new one (really a job for the tradesman); the installation of the Electro Osmosis system (which any Rentokil representative will tell you all about); one of the other types of contractor-installed methods; or brush treatment, applied by you.

There is a material called Stroma. This is a damp-repellent material which, when brushed on the wall, will penetrate up to 9 in. of brick. You apply it both inside and out and it will hold back rising damp effectively. This is not a job for a silicone repellent.

Finally, the bridged damp-proof course. So often, piles of sand, earth or even rockeries are allowed to heap up above course level, allowing damp into the wall at danger-height. Once this happens, the damp-proof course will prevent the damp from escaping downwards. So keep it free from all obstructions. It should be at least 6 in. above ground level – bear this in mind, particularly if you lay a concrete path. So many folk bring the path level up to the damp-proof course, then wonder why splashes of water cause the wall to become damp.

DAMP FLOORS

Persistent damp in wood (suspended type) floors not only seriously affects the floor itself and the floor coverings, but presents a threat to the structural soundness of the house itself. You see, damp timber is an open invitation to dry rot spores which are always present in the air. The spores, once given a foothold on wet timber, rapidly grow to form large, mushroom-like growths, which then enable the fungus to spread like wildfire through all the other timber in the house, damp or not. Brickwork is no barrier to the spread of the fungus, so it could also attack your neighbour's house.

Soon, the attacked timber becomes brittle. Cracks appear across the grain and the wood crumbles, but you can recognise the attack by a number of symptoms. There will be a damp, musty smell; wood will warp and crack; you will be able to dig a penknife blade easily into the timber. If you lift floorboards you will see whitish, cobweb-like strands and, somewhere, a foul-looking, mushroom-like growth.

Once this stage has been reached it is best to call in an expert to confirm your diagnosis and advise about effective treatment. It is unlikely that you will be able to deal with the problem *effectively* yourself, for every trace of infection must be destroyed; all affected timber must be cut out and destroyed by burning, and surrounding areas must be sterilised so that another attack will not occur.

Dealing with the damp – preferably before dry rot attacks – is usually a fairly simple matter. The main cause of a build-up is lack of ventilation. Some people block the ventilation holes during the winter months in order to conserve heat, but this is the worst possible thing to do. Keep them clear, and make sure that there are plenty of them!

When timber has to be replaced, either because of damp or after an attack of dry rot, we strongly recommend that you insist on specially treated timber. True, it does cost a bit more than the untreated variety, but it is protected for life against both rot and insect attack. In our view, it should be compulsory for all new timber installed where fungus and insect attack is likely, to be treated in this way; just take a look around new housing estates to see untreated timber being used in such places – paring pence on the price of the house only to leave the new owner with troubles at a later date.

Wet rot is nowhere near so serious. It can be caused when timber gets really soaked and stays that way for some time. It may be because you have a leak in your plumbing system.

Wet rot will only darken the wood, make it soft and push off paint coatings. But it will not spread in the same way as dry rot. Here you can cut out the affected timber and replace it. Again, use treated timber for the replacement.

Going upwards slightly from the floor itself, skirting boards attacked by damp should be removed, treated or renewed, and replaced using new timber plugs set in the wall. It is a good idea here to put some Protim fungicidal plugs in the wall before replacing the skirting board. These are sticks of solid fungicide which stay put until damp appears. Then they slowly dissolve, killing off any fungus spores which may be present. In this way you get a first-class form of protection for an area you cannot see and where dry rot may get a hold.

Apart from natural damp, it is worth while keeping an eye on your plumbing and central heating systems for leaks. Lift loose floorcovering occasionally, particularly vinyls, and check for signs of damp. Occasionally check the space under your suspended floor; if you find a persistent pool of water there, which is not due to a leaking pipe, have a word with your local borough surveyor. He will give you advice on what to do about it.

CHAPTER SEVEN
Noise, Draughts, Ventilation and Cold

NOISE

One of the major problems of modern life is noise and, if anything, it is on the increase. Most of us learn to put up with noise while we are out and about, but once the front door is shut we all have the right to a bit of peace and quiet. Unfortunately, lots of people don't get it.

Traffic passing the house or aircraft flying overhead is one type, but by far the most common complaint concerns noise through a party wall – in a terraced or semi-detached house. Or noise from a flat above. Radio sets, television and really powerful hi-fi sets are the real culprits, but unfortunately many modern houses built to the minimum standards to keep costs down are just piling on the agony.

Party walls are skimpy; living rooms and bedrooms adjoin – and there are cases where toilets adjoin next door's main bedroom so that even the toilet paper can be heard rustling! This is absolutely deplorable, and if you are waiting for a new semi to be built, have a good look at the layout. There is no reason at all why passages and non-living areas should not be arranged so that noise is cut to a minimum.

Let's look at the party wall – the wall shared by two houses. It can be built with a cavity so that you have in fact two close detached homes, but as one large builder said, this adds to the cost. I wonder how it compares with the cost of a nervous breakdown? Unfortunately, only part of the noise comes straight through the party wall. Noise also passes into adjoining walls, floors and ceilings, all of which pass the noise to your home!

What can be done? Well, it *is* often difficult, but the best remedy is to be on good terms with your neighbours. If you talk things over at the outset you can often reduce noise level.

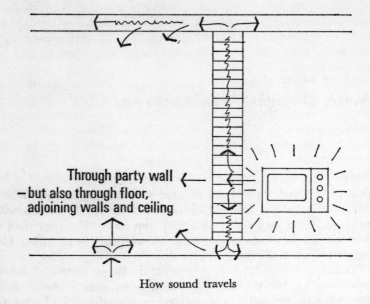

How sound travels

Televisions, radios and especially hi-fi equipment should never be sited on the party wall. You will often hear programmes as loud as they do! If they are sited on the far side of the room, or even in another room not adjoining your living room, the level will be greatly reduced.

Soft linings help muffle noise before it passes into the wall, so thick curtains, upholstered furniture, ceiling tiles and a deep pile carpet will keep your noise in your room to a certain extent. You can prove this for yourself when you enter an empty house. Listen how the noise reverberates around the house.

Assuming you get no co-operation, what then? Well, as far as we know there is no cheap way of reducing noise. First, remember that materials that insulate against cold do not necessarily help with noise. In fact, to kill noise you need dense, thick materials such as brick or block. Expanded polystyrene is next to useless.

So, a new brick or block wall about 6 in. to 8 in. from the existing wall is best; but you can imagine the difficulties involved in building it A compromise is 2 in. square timber fixed to the wall, floor to ceiling, and spaced about 1 ft. 2 in. apart. Fill the gaps between the timber lengths with glass-fibre blanket then cover the lot with sheet plasterboard. The plasterboard must not touch adjoining walls, floor or ceilings, but should be separated by a wodge of glass fibre. This is to stop noise being transmitted into the plasterboard, which can then act as a sounding board.

You can then decorate the plasterboard. Another possibility is to build a wall of wardrobes in a bedroom, giving you a sealed air space full of sound-deadening clothes, or in a lounge, timber panelling with insulation between battens will help a little. Even a wall of booksheves can help a bit – but do remember that all these treatments bring only minimal relief.

When it comes to ceilings and floors, combined efforts win again. The tramp of feet above, or the click of heels, can best be killed by a thick underlay and carpet. Adding ceiling tiles does very little. In really serious cases a false floor is the only answer, with dry sand packed between the two layers. But this is a job for the tradesman.

Noise may come in from outside if you live near a main road. Double glazing can help provided you bear in mind that the stuff sold for heat insulation has little effect unless the spacing between panes is 6 in. to 8 in. It is also advisable for the two panes to be of different weights of glass. If your panes are closer than 2 in., the sound insulating effect is no better than having one piece of glass twice as thick.

Gaps and cracks are the worst offenders, so see that all holes are sealed. And, of course, opening a window kills any insulation you may have installed. That is why there is growing interest in ventilation units designed to admit air to a room while special in-built baffles filter out all noise.

Incidentally, if you want more information on noise in relation to glazing, drop a line to the Insulation Glazing Association, 6 Mount Row, London, W1Y 6DY, and ask for a free copy of their leaflet, *Windows and Noise*.

You can also reduce noise level from a busy road by some form of barrier, such as a privet hedge or fence sited well away from the house, but don't expect too much in the way of results. Where a noise is really getting on top of you – as with perhaps unreasonable neighbours – remember it is an offence. A chat with your local police could well lead to a caution or, at worst, a prosecution. But when things reach this stage, it really is time to move.

DOUBLE GLAZING

Double glazing has definite benefits. It will kill lots of draughts around window frames; it can considerably reduce condensation under set conditions. And it will eliminate the convected air currents which make sitting near single-glazed windows very unpleasant in winter.

It is also important to keep a sense of proportion. Reading some of the literature put out by some of the less reputable companies you would think double glazing solves everything. 'Save 50 per cent of your heat loses', says the blurb – but it doesn't point out that the 50 per cent refers to window area only. On the average house, this is about 20 per cent of the exterior surface, so the actual saving is 50 per cent of 20 per cent, which is 10 per cent.

So, if you spend £300 on having your home double glazed and your heating bill was £100 a year, you will save £10 a year. Thus, it will take you 30 years to recoup the cost of double glazing, assuming you stay in the house that long. It wants consideration, doesn't it?

Of course we're not advocating ignoring double glazing, but it may be worth just doing certain windows, or adopting a D.I.Y. scheme which will cost far less than getting a firm in to do it. A rough guide to the types of double glazing follows, but if you want details of companies, drop a line to the Insulation Glazing Association, 6 Mount Row, London, W1Y 6DY.

Simplest of all – and least attractive – is thin transparent sheeting held in place with double sided tape. Or the sheet can be sandwiched between battens used to make a simple frame, then held in place by clips. This system is ideal in locations where appearance doesn't matter too much, for however well you secure the sheeting, you will still know the sheet is there by the reflections off it.

Flexible plastic channelling offers a simple way of double glazing. The plastic is mitred to fit around a sheet of glass, so the glass actually supports the plastic frame. Then the unit is held in place by plastic clips screwed to the window frame. A useful system where it is possible to store the units during the better weather.

Next comes rigid plastic or metal frames where the frame really supports the glass. This obviously makes for more rigid frames, but cost goes up too. The frame may be removable, or it may be hinged or set to run in a sliding channel. This is the system most used by the tailor-made companies.

A simple D.I.Y. method involves only timber beading, and the extra sheet of glass is held permanently in place by beading cushioned with mastic. A common complaint here is that moisture condenses between panes, then you can't get at it. Silica gel crystals place between panes can help, but you really need to get these out occasionally to dry them out, thus re-energising them. Another way to reduce condensation is to drill fine holes to the outside air – which is usually drier than air inside the house, even on a damp day.

The most reliable system involves the use of factory-sealed units, some of which can be used in existing window frames while others need a special deep rebate. Some units offered are made to fit standard frames; others are produced to individual requirements. And of course they are dearer than many systems – about four times the cost of normal window glass. Obviously, the ideal time to install such units is when the house is being built. In this way you don't have to throw out any existing glass.

Now a security note. Double glazing offers protection against the burglar who likes knocking a hole in a window so he can reach the catch. He will normally leave double-glazed frames well alone.

CAVITY INSULATION

The cavity was a great idea in one respect. It stopped damp getting from outside to inside as it couldn't bridge the gap between the two wall leaves. But it created a problem, for with air flowing freely in the cavity, warmth from the house was lost via the air flow. So architects argued for years on whether the cavity should be blocked off or not, and it is only in recent years that the boffins have come up with a solution. Fill the cavity with insulation.

The material chosen was foamed plastic, which won't hold damp, is fire-resistant and will not allow damp to rise by capillary action. The plastic is foamed in a special tank taken to the job, and once it comes into contact with the air, it starts to harden.

Well, that's the idea, but is it worth it? The simple answer is yes, because the area through which heat can escape is considerable. It has been proved that just filling the cavity with foam can reduce annual fuel consumption by 20 per cent. And that means 20p saving in every £1 spent on fuel. Combine this with good loft insulation you could cut heat loses by 50 per cent. And that doesn't include double glazing.

As for the actual job, many folk are hesitant in case the work is messy. In fact it isn't. Holes are drilled at set intervals in the exterior walls, and pieces of stick pushed in. Then foam is pumped in and the sticks are watched. When they move, it indicates where the foam has reached them and whether a given area is full. Then the nozzle is moved.

When the wall is complete, air vents are poked clear, then the holes sealed with a matching mortar. Unless you get very close to the wall, it is impossible to see where the holes have been.

Can the foam make a mess indoors? It is possible if there is a gap somewhere, but most unlikely. And anyway the foam does not spoil anything, as it hardens very quickly. What does it cost? An average three-bedroom house, semi-detached, will cost between £100 and £150 to be treated. And the job will be completed easily in a day.

If you are having a new place built, the ideal time to get the foam put in is when the walls are up to height. It is obviously far easier to see what is going on at this stage, and no holes need be drilled in the walls. And if you have this job done during building, the improved insulation value of the walls will affect your central heating system. You will need a smaller boiler and less area of radiators, and you could save a fair bit of what you spend on the infill right at the outset.

Where can you contact a firm doing this work? The Yellow Pages is probably the best bet. Or you will find firms advertise in local papers. But whoever you choose, make sure it is a reputable company which will guarantee the work. If in any doubt, ask them to put you in touch with two or three people who have had the job done. No reputable company will mind.

Can this be a do-it-yourself job? Well, the usual answer is no, but we have heard of a group of men who hired equipment from one of the larger firms and did their own homes, saving themselves a fair bit of cash. But before a company would allow you to do this, they would expect you to attend a training course to learn how to use the expensive equipment properly.

NOISE, DRAUGHTS, VENTILATION AND COLD

Incidentally, Rentokil have added cavity infill to the list of jobs they tackle, but they don't use foam. They blow a fibrous insulation material into the cavity by air pressure. Any local agent will give you a guide to their prices.

If you plan to insulate this winter, take a tip from us, and put cavity infill at the top of the list.

DRAUGHTS

Whatever precautions you have taken to keep your home warm during the cold weather, and whatever insulation you have applied to plumbing and house fabric; success will depend very much on how draught-free your house is. Gaps and cracks which are of no consequence during warm weather become vitally important when the air blowing in is of sub-zero temperatures. No form of insulation can withstand an icy blast for long.

Draughts near the plumbing system are of course the ones to find first. Examine overflow pipes from tanks and cisterns, for very often cold air can blow straight up the pipes and into a vital spot. Entry can be stopped by small, loose-swinging flaps designed to fit to the exposed end of an overflow pipe. Wind force will close it, but it will soon open again when water pours down. Alternatively, carry the inner end of the overflow pipe to just below water level in the tank or cistern so that air is unable to enter.

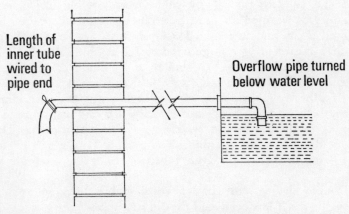

Two methods of preventing freezing draughts through the overflow pipe

Another vital spot is the discharge gully where waste pipes from basins and bath in upper rooms meet. It pays to build a simple box, or at least a shelter of bituminous felt or vinyl plastic to keep the wind off.

Then have a look in the loft and feel for draughts at the eaves. In some older plumbing systems, rising pipes were sited near unprotected eaves, so no wonder this is the spot where many pipes freeze. If you feel draughts here, stuff the eaves, where roof and floor meet, with mineral wool or glass fibre.

Again, in older properties, the roof may be unfelted, meaning you can see daylight between the tiles. This means that loft temperature will probably equal the outside air temperature! In this case you can at least pin a waterproof building paper to the rafters, then feed the end of the paper as far out at the eaves as you can. This is to ensure that in-blown snow or rain is carried out of the roof space.

Look also in larders and store cupboards which have ventilation bricks. Cover them over for the winter.

Having said that, don't stop the draught entering outside air bricks at damp-proof course level. These must be left open so that air can circulate under the floor. If you stop this air, you stand a good chance of encouraging an attack of dry rot. It loves damp, still, conditions, but hates a draught!

Draughts will also rob you of the value of house heating, for you can be sure that if icy cold air is blowing in, an equal quantity of warmed air must be going out somewhere. So check around doors and windows, for those tiny gaps soon add up to an area representing a large window full open all the time! Use phosphor bronze strip, or similar strip made of plastic, for exterior doors. Use the same strip for casement windows, or use a self-adhesive foam plastic strip in such a way that the window frame beds on to it. Strips are available for clipping on to metal frames, or there are types which can be riveted in place. Don't forget the letter-box opening. It's amazing how much draught can come in there! It's even worth fitting a flap over the keyhole.

Double glazing can be of considerable help in reducing draughts for it has been said that in many cases the glazing does more good in killing draughts than it does in retaining heat.

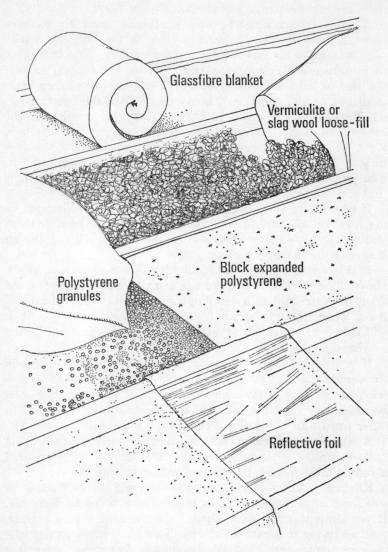

Five methods of insulating a loft floor

Seal gaps at the bases of doors too. For exterior doors there are special weather bars and water traps. And for interior doors there are various patterns of rise and fall excluder.

A word of warning. Certain appliances need air to burn correctly, and if your draught-proofing is first class, you may need to supply air especially for the appliance. The best place to introduce an air supply is either side of the hearth, as near the fire or appliance as possible. There are proprietary vents available, or you can bore a hole either side of the hearth yourself if you have timber floors. Do mind any gas pipes or electric cables. Oh, and mind your eyes when your bit gets through, for a jet of cold air can shoot out, blowing dust and shavings in your face. Fit a bit of gauze over the vents to keep out dirt. The proprietary ones have this too, and they have the advantage that you can close them if you wish.

If your floors are solid, fit a small ventilator just above skirting level on an outside wall, as near the fire as possible. You will find that your new vents will supply the fire with all the air it needs without causing icy draughts.

If this method is impossible, then the place to leave a gap is above door level. Either leave a gap along the top edge of the door, or better still fit a ventilator in that bit of wall above the door. Then, should the air from outside the room be cold, it will mix with warmed air at ceiling level in the room before moving down to the fire.

If you do a fair bit of entertaining, or if a number of folk in the family smoke, above-door ventilators are a good idea anyway, for if there is no air movement in a room, the air soon becomes stale, and the inmates will be noticeably lethargic. In other words, an unventilated room can be unhealthy.

A sensible arrangement is to see that the air in the adjoining hall or passage is warm too, so that if a door is left ajar, or if a ventilator is opened, no one will notice anyway.

Kitchen ventilation needs a bit of thought, too, especially if you have a good extractor fan fitted, and a boiler in there too. If you draughtproof the kitchen, then put your fan on extract, you are trying to create a vacuum. This is definitely against the laws of nature, and air will be drawn down the boiler flue (together with fumes and smoke!) to replace that being extracted. To prevent this, fit a floor ventilator fairly near the boiler, and let that feed the boiler and correct any differences

NOISE, DRAUGHTS, VENTILATION AND COLD

of pressure. The only snag is of course that you will be pulling in very cold air to replace the nice warm air you are pushing outside. This is where a charcoal filter fan unit scores, for the in-built fan draws stale, moist air over the filter, then recirculates it in the room, with no loss of temperature, and no pull of cold air in. The filters can be washed at regular intervals to remove grease and other deposits.

Another distinct advantage of floor ventilators is that you improve underfloor ventilation, thus further reducing the chances of rot.

If you live near one of our noisy airports, before you plan a ventilation scheme, be sure to ask your local council for details of possible grants towards the fitting of air conditioning plant. Units are available which admit fresh air but block out most outside noise.

Finally, if you have an old open type fire, enquire at your local housewarming centre for information on throat restrictors. It may be you could restrict the throat above the fire considerably without affecting its efficiency, yet by doing this, you will drastically reduce the pull of air up the flue – which in turn will reduce the amount of air needed to feed it. Another draught gone!

FREEZE-UP

When sub-zero temperatures descend upon us for a few weeks, many still expect our way of living to grind to a freezing halt – not only on the roads, but in the home too. If only folk took a few elementary steps, our homes could continue as normal, despite the efforts of a previous generation of plumbers to place vital pipes in places where they must freeze!

The most annoying thing is when the supply pipe to your house freezes. This really shouldn't happen, but if it does, it is worth checking to see if the supply pipe is the regulation minimum of 2 ft. 6 in. below ground level. If not, notify your local water board and ask their advice. They also have gear for defreezing a supply pipe.

Check on pipes which run up the inside of exterior walls. These are very prone to freezing because of heat loss. If possible, ease the pipe from the wall just enough to push a piece of wood so that the pipe is not in contact with the wall. And if you have boxed-in pipes, do be sure to leave a gap, top and bottom, so warm air can circulate. You may well cause a freeze if you insulate the pipes from the warmth of the room.

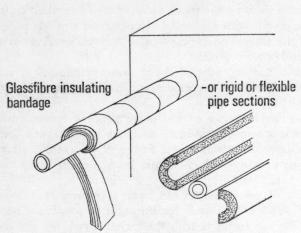

Two ways to keep plumbing pipework warm

Check all stop taps and make sure they can be turned on and off easily – even by the children. Dad is sure to be out when emergency action is called for! And know which ones turn off what now. Don't wait until you haven't time to find out.

Good general lagging is, of course, essential, both of cold tanks and pipes, and including the expansion pipe which bends over above the cold tank. An ice block in this pipe could lead to an explosion in certain circumstances. A tubular heater of the black heat type, operating at 60 watts per ft. will keep the chill off a loft, and you can buy a special cold tank immersion heater to keep the chill off the water in the tank – but remember these heaters must be put on before a freeze-up, not after. Never use oil heaters or reflector type heaters in the loft. There is a risk of fire.

Remember that no insulation can resist cold indefinitely, however good it is. So if you have an outside toilet, even a small heater such as a paraffin car heater, an oil lantern, a candle in a jar – or even a 25 watt lamp left on – will make just a degree or so of difference, provided the room is draught-free. For surer protection, use heating cable or heating tapes wound around vital pipes. These must of course be on in good time.

In the house, avoid dripping taps – a most common cause of frozen waste pipes and outside gullies. If a tap drips, put the plug in the basin or sink until you can replace the washer. If you do get a frozen waste pipe, don't waste time pouring water into the bath or basin. Get outside with a kettle of boiling water and pour it over the pipes where they come out of the wall.

Water in a lavatory pan can be prevented from freezing by tipping a handful of salt in the water in the pan; or if you go away for a few days, by pushing a piece of rubber or plastic tubing into the bend. Should water freeze, pressure of expansion is taken up by the tube, not by the pan.

If you do get a minor freeze in a pipe, apply hot rags or the heat from a hair dryer to the pipe. The sooner you do it, the smaller the ice plug you have to melt. Never, never use a blowlamp, for while you may thaw the pipe, you may burn down your home in the process!

To effect temporary repairs should a pipe burst, keep a glass fibre repair kit of the type that contains glass fibre bandage. Provided you can get the damaged section dry by draining that pipe or turning off the water to it, you can make a perfect repair that will withstand full pressure in a very short time.

Now finally, if you must leave your home for any length of time, remember that no insulation can withstand low temperatures indefinitely. It is far safer to drain your water system before you go away, then you are sure no harm can come to it. Remember just running taps will not drain hot tank and boiler. You should find a drain cock on or near your boiler and, if you are lucky, there may be one by the hot water cylinder. If you have central heating, you will find drain cocks at the lowest points in the system and, before you try to drain, don't forget to turn the water off at the mains!

It has been argued that despite this, there will still be a column of water in the mains feed pipe going up to the cold water storage tank. This is true, but the only way you can drain this is to fit a drain cock to it just above the mains stop tap. Failing that, if you have a heating tape or cable, or a portable black heat tubular heater, position it near the mains pipe.

CHAPTER EIGHT
Plumbing

CENTRAL HEATING
Most of a plumbing system will function year in, year out, without attention. But it would be very unwise to ignore a central heating system from one winter to the next. A check at least once a year, before the new heating season starts, is a minimum. A number of heating firms will do a simple overhaul for a fee, or, if you use gas, you can take out a service agreement with your local gas board. This costs under £10 a year, split over the quarterly bills. For this you get a major check, plus a further check during the winter running period.

Apart from boiler and flue, it is worth your while checking around the system for leaks. Rub your fingers around pipe joints looking for tell-tale weeps. Constant expansion and contraction may have caused slight looseness, and a quarter turn with a spanner on compression joints may be all that is required. Never put too much pressure on or you may cause damage.

If a weep persists, loosen off the joint a couple of turns, apply Boss White to the thread and retighten. If this fails, you will have to break the joint. If the joint is on a pipe run, you will have to drain down that part of the system, but if it is at a radiator, this is not necessary, but be prepared for a bit of mess.

Place a shallow dish under the joint and turn off the control valve attached to the joint. This may be the on-off control, or it may be the valve at the other end of a radiator which has a cover over it. If the latter, undo the screw holding the cover, take it off, then close the valve with a screwdriver or a spanner.

Now you need a cork to plug the radiator. Slacken off the nut, pull the joint open and push the cork in place. Smear the joint thread with Boss White or use ptfe tape to bind the thread. Now nip the cork out and remake the joint. You will spill some water, so be prepared, for it probably won't be very clean.

Check radiators for leaks. Those good old-fashioned cast-iron ones may have looked grim, but they lasted for ever. The modern wafer-thin steel ones look elegant, but they can very quickly rust away. If you find pinholes in a radiator, it is best not to mess about. It probably needs replacing. You cannot repair a hole with the rad full of water, either with solder or epoxy based filler.

To drain the radiator, you need to turn off the control valve either side, slacken off the vent plug located at a top end so air can get in, then loosen off a joint. Have plenty of receptacles handy to collect the water, and again be prepared for it to be dirty. With the water drained off, undo both pipe joints and lift the radiator from its brackets.

If one radiator has pinholes, check the others too. It is advisable to put an additive in your system such as Fernox. This completely protects the system against corrosion. It costs a few pounds, but it is a good investment. The chemical can be added any time by tipping it into the central heating header tank in the loft.

Tie up the ball arm so no new water can enter the tank, then drain off a gallon or so by the drain cock at the lowest point in the system. You will find the level has dropped to nil in the little tank (or it should do) – which means the chemical has moved into the system. Don't forget to release the ball arm when you're finished.

PLUMBING SYSTEM

A plumbing system is a wonderful thing. It goes on year after year with no attention, until suddenly there's big trouble. So a spare hour spent checking things over is very worth while just before winter.

Check all stop taps. The most important is the one on the mains supply – probably tucked under the kitchen sink. It's a fair bet it hasn't been touched in years, and that the weaker members of the household can't even begin to turn it off! Yet that's the one to shut quickly if you get trouble. Apply easing oil and turn it on and off until it is easy. Now check any others on feed pipes elsewhere in the system.

Look at the house taps. Any drips? Hard to turn off? Replace old washers and, if the actual tap seating is worn, you

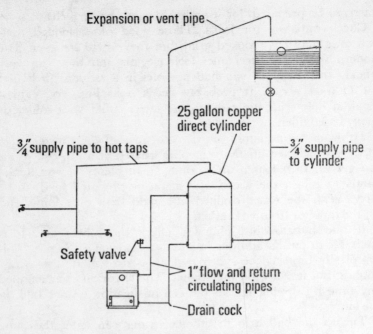

DIRECT PLUMBING SYSTEM

Above, and facing page: basic plumbing systems

can get nylon seatings and washers which will make an old tap as good as new. Look for drips coming out of the handle, especially when a hose connection is used. It probably means that the packing needs boosting a bit. Try tightening the packing nut a little. If this fails, you will have to remove the nut and put in a bit more packing. Knitting wool smeared with Vaseline is ideal.

Examine the ball valve in the toilet cistern. If yours is an old house, it may pay you to replace the ball with a new plastic one. Is there a silencer tube leading down into the water from the valve? If not, you can buy a plastic tube for a matter of pence. It is wise to see that the tube has a hole near the top to prevent back-siphoning of water should the water supply fail. The tank in the loft will also need attention (see page 145).

Have you central heating? Well, you may be covered by a

PLUMBING

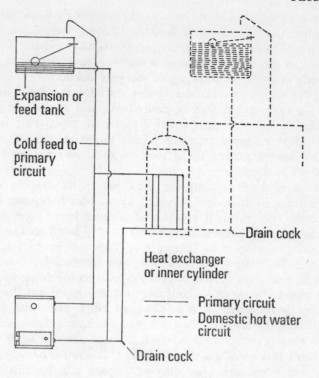

INDIRECT SYSTEM

regular annual or bi-annual service. If not, do give everything a check over before the system is put to work for the winter, as mentioned earlier. If yours is a direct system where the water heated is that used domestically and to heat the radiators, you may benefit from a descaling session. Kits can be bought to enable you to do this job yourself very simply and with no mess. Scale does cut down efficiency. If you have an indirect system, it is a good idea to invest in an additive for the radiator circuit (see page 137). Check the valves and compression joints for drips and that no air is trapped in radiators situated at high points. And what about frost protection. Is your system O.K.? (see Chapter 7).

COPPER PIPEWORK
The preserves of the tradesman plumber were safe from all but

the keenest handyman as long as the plumber's work involved lead pipe and wiped joints. But the introduction of small bore copper pipe and simple jointing methods has changed all that. If you can use a tape measure, a hacksaw and a spanner, there is a wide range of plumbing jobs you can tackle.

Copper tube is by far the easiest stuff for the handyman to use. It is easily cut to length, easily bent, and very easily joined to plumbing fittings and other lengths of pipe. You have a choice of three main types of joints; non-manipulative, manipulative and capillary. Let's look at each in turn, and don't be put off by the names.

Non-manipulative joints are those where no shaping of the copper tube is necessary provided an absolutely square end is cut on the tube ends. If you intend doing a lot of pipe cutting, get a small pipe cutter. This is only a little hand tool and you can get a good one for about £1. This will ensure that the ends are dead true. After cutting, any internal burr must be removed, and most cutters have a shaped end for doing this.

To make the joint, a coupling nut is slipped on the tube, and this is followed by a soft copper ring. The tube is then pushed into the body of the joint, and the nut is tightened. The copper ring is compressed between the nut and the body of the joint, and this gives a watertight joint. It should be noted that under real stress, this joint may pull apart, and for this reason it is not usually allowed by water authorities for underground work.

Manipulative joints are those where the tube ends have to be shaped, or manipulated, to take the joint. Because the tube is shaped, such joints will not pull apart under stress, so this is the joint for underground installations.

The actual shaping of the pipe is not a difficult job, as the firm producing the joints also make a tool to perform this operation. The tool is inserted in the pipe end, and, as the tool is turned, a hardened steel ball rises and makes a ridge around the pipe not far from the end. When turned the other way, the tool can be withdrawn. With larger orders of fittings, the makers supply a tool free of charge, but on small orders, they make a charge which is refunded when the tool is returned to them. Or, if you prefer, you can buy the tool to keep.

The third type of joint is the capillary, and there are a number of advantages with this one. First, it is much neater as no nuts are necessary. Second, as there are no nuts, they can be fixed close to walls or floors where it would be impossible to get a spanner. And third, they are a lot cheaper than the other types. But there is one disadvantage in that you need a blowtorch or blowlamp, so a little more skill and care is necessary. A large piece of asbestos cloth is a must to avoid scorching surrounding materials.

The joint relies for its seal on a ring of solder incorporated in the joint. The tube is cleaned, flux is applied to the tube and to the inside of the fitting, the tube is inserted in the fitting, then heat is applied until a complete ring of solder appears around the mouth of the fitting. This solder has in fact been drawn into the narrow space between pipe and fitting by capillary attraction, hence the name of the fitting. The joint is allowed to cool, and that is all there is to it.

If you want to know more, have a chat with your local plumbers merchants. They will show you the fittings and perhaps be able to give you a catalogue dealing with the type you choose. If not, the manufacturer concerned can supply one.

PLASTICS IN PLUMBING

There have been tremendous developments in the use of plastics in recent years, particularly in the domestic field. And no part of the home has been more affected and transformed than the good old British plumbing.

Probably first in the field was the nylon tap seating and washer. This consists of a plastic jumper and washer combined, plus a plastic collar designed to push down on to an existing tap seating. If the seating is worn or damaged, the collar will give it a new lease of life, and the two items combined give very effective service.

Plastic sink tops have not so far been very successful. The glass fibre type tends to delaminate with the changes in temperature which a sink must take. Both Perspex and glass fibre sinks are easily scratched, they are affected by certain chemicals and certainly by really hot articles. Plastic waste traps, however, are here to stay, and they greatly simplify the job of keeping the U-trap clean, as most plastic traps are easily dismantled for cleaning.

Plastic water pipe is common now, but at the moment only for cold water services. Pipes to carry hot water are being developed, but that is for the future. Plastic pipe is extremely easy to assemble, and, provided that the pipe is given good support, it will give no trouble. It cannot be damaged by frost, of course, but there is just one slight disadvantage. It does not conduct electricity, so you cannot earth to plastic pipe.

Moving to the toilet, you can now get all-plastic cisterns, and very effective they are, with their silent flushing and non-corrosive parts. If you have a perfectly good lavatory cistern, you could fit a plastic ball float if the metal one packs up. This may be either a hollow plastic sphere, or a solid lump of expanded polystyrene. Both are equally effective.

Plastic baths are gaining in popularity. They are available in a most attractive range of colours, are extremely light in weight and easy to fit. They do need more support than the old type of bath, but most manufacturers provide a cradle for the bath, sometimes utilising the crate in which it is sent. You must take reasonable care of your plastic bath. No harsh abrasive, no cigarette ends rested on the lip and no chemicals such as paint stripper or brush cleaner spilt in it.

There are plenty of plastic shower fittings, too, including simple units designed to fit over a bath, with plastic shower curtains which drape into the bath – through to plastic shower cabinets complete with fittings. One firm has even introduced a plastic bathroom moulded in one piece and supplied with fittings – all ready to be dropped into a new house.

For the garden, there is plastic pipe and plastic taps which will never be affected by frost, even if they do temporarily freeze in severe weather. And plastic garden hose, though it does tend to stiffen in colder weather. Finally, no plastic plumbing system would be complete without a new plastic cold water cistern in the loft (see page 146).

TAPS AND WASHERS

If a tap starts to drip, don't ignore it, especially during freezing weather, for those drips can very soon cause a blockage in a waste pipe. And don't get into the habit of merely forcing the tap off really tight. You will chew up the old washer, and you may score the seating. Change the washer. It is simple enough.

Cut off the water supply to the tap. With cold taps that are mains fed, the mains stop cock, usually in the kitchen, will do fine. Other taps may be isolated by a further stop tap on supply pipes, but failing that you will have to drain off the tank feeding the tap.

Older taps are a little easier to deal with. On a modern tap there may be an easy-clean cover. To get the cover off, you will need to undo the grub screw holding the handle, then the cover can be unscrewed and removed. If it is stubborn, do be careful not to damage the chromium plating. Often a strip of old leather strap, or even a length of coarse string, wound tightly around the cover, will offer sufficient purchase to enable you to turn the cover.

Screw the tap open as far as you can, then apply a wrench to the flat faces on the head gear. You need a second wrench to hold the tap body firm so that when you apply pressure to one wrench, you can equal it with the other. If you don't do this, you may well have a broken basin to replace as well as a washer!

In the base of the head gear you will see the bit called the jumper, and, at its base, the old washer. The nut on this part will probably be very difficult to remove, due to corrosion or hard water deposit. If it proves impossible, throw away the old jumper and get a new one ready fitted with a washer. The cost will be very small.

Now what about the washer type? Most will be $\frac{1}{2}$ in. diameter, but bath taps may be $\frac{3}{4}$ in. When getting a new washer, state whether it is for a hot or cold tap. They can vary in composition. Get a few spares while you are at it.

With the new washer on, before you put the tap together again, put your finger in the tap and feel the valve seating. It should be smooth and free from pits or projections. If it feels in any way rough, this may well be the cause of damage to the old washer. If you are not able to grind the face, you can buy a new nylon seating, and a jumper and washer unit too, called the Evans Full Stop seating and jumper. These are very easily fitted, and they will give the tap a new lease of life.

If all is well, Vaseline the tap threads and screw together again. Incidentally, if drips of water come out of the tap by the spindle, a part turn on the gland adjuster screw should do the trick, as it will force the gland packing into tighter contact with the spindle.

The information so far given does not apply to the Supatap. This is specially designed so that the tap can be screwed right open and the washer renewed without turning off the water at all. We're not going to give a lengthy description of how to do this, for any ironmonger who stocks these taps should be able to give you an illustrated leaflet which shows just how the job is done.

A final tip. When changing a washer over bath or basin, first put the plug in the waste. Grub screws seem to be magnetically attracted to wastes! And secondly, put plenty of clothes in the bath or sink to deaden the impact when you drop your wrench! You would be amazed how many times a plumber is called in to deal with an accident which started as a washer changing operation.

BALL VALVES

The ball valve is the part of a plumbing system we take most for granted. It is virtually an automatic tap which switches on and off hundreds of times, year after year, with no attention. Its purpose is to allow the replacement of water in the storage tank and lavatory cisterns.

But why, you may ask, can't taps and toilets be fed straight from the mains anyway? In many districts this is in fact done, but in densely populated areas such as London it is not allowed. Storage tanks act as a buffer against times of peak demand when pipes would literally be drained dry if all taps were mains-fed. Also, the storage tank acts as an emergency supply for those rare occasions when the water is cut off. But let's get back to the ball valve. Where are they situated?

You will find one in the storage tank, probably in the loft, operating at mains pressure. Then you will find one in each lavatory cistern, and this may be operating at mains pressure in certain districts, or it may be working merely on the head of water from the storage tank. It is essential to know which you have if you ever get around to replacing the ball unit, for we have heard of more than one faulty ball valve which merely turned out to be the wrong valve unit for the pressure available.

There are three main types of valve. The old Croydon valve which tends to be rather noisy and to which you cannot fit a silencer tube (this is a tube designed to feed water below water line, thus reducing noise.) The Portsmouth valve, also a common one, has an outlet threaded to take a silencer tube. The latest Garston ball valve is the most silent of the valves, and it allows very rapid refilling of a cistern. If you fit one of these to replace an old Portsmouth pattern, you may be disappointed that there is still a little noise. But this is likely to be because the cistern will refill in half the time, and the extra volume of water on the move makes the noise.

The valve is operated by a ball float, and on older models this will be of copper, which is liable to corrode. Incidentally, if yours becomes holed, as an emergency repair, slip a sound polythene bag over the emptied ball and secure with string. Simple, but effective.

Today, you can get either hollow plastic ball floats, or expanded plastic floats which are virtually solidified foam. And they may be square instead of round. Whatever the shape, they will give less trouble. On the older models, however, the arm connecting valve and float was of softish metal and, to get the water to the right level (a mark on the cistern side), you have to bend the arm very carefully up or down. More modern arms have adjustment simply by means of a wing or knurled nut.

Washer replacement is easy, provided that you can get the securing pins out; they tend to get corroded. The new Garston pattern is extremely easy to get to pieces to get at the rubber diaphragm, which should give years of wear anyway. So, if your valves are noisy or are getting old, replace them. The job will cost very little.

TANK IN THE LOFT

Out of sight, out of mind. That's the poor old cold water storage tank in many a loft. It goes year after year without so much as a glance – until one day there is water coming through a ceiling! So a periodic check of the tank is well worth while. Tie up the ball valve arm, run water until the tank runs dry, then mop out the remainder of the water which will still be trapped below the level of the outflow pipe. This pipe should be set up a few inches so that sediment does not pour out.

It's not a bad idea to dry the inside of the tank with a blow torch to get it really dry. Scrape off any deposits, treat rusted patches with a cold galvanising paint, then coat the inside of the tank with at least two coats of non-tainting bituminous paint. A special paint is available for this kind of job. It is advisable to plug off pipes connected to the tank while doing this work so that sediments cannot pass into the pipes. Pieces of broom handle sharpened to a rough point make good plugs.

If the tank is in a pretty poor state, you can now get special plastic tank liners which are inserted into the tank, so that the old tank is used only as a support for the liner. This can add years of life to an otherwise useless tank. Any good plumbers merchant should be able to give you more details.

If you have put in a new galvanised tank, a device called a sacrificial anode can fully protect the tank against corrosion. The anode is a special block of metal which is connected to the tank by a clip, the anode being suspended in the water. Now the effect is that electrolytic action will cause the anode to dissolve away rather than the galvanising on your tank. When the anode has dissolved, you need to put in a new one.

With the tank in good shape, how is the ball valve? If it is old and worn, fit a Garston pattern ball valve. Make sure that you get a high pressure model. And while you are at it, fit a plastic ball float. Metal ones also corrode and, if the ball fills up, you could have a flood.

If you need a new tank, get one of the new circular black plastic tanks. They have the advantage that the tank can be compressed to push it through quite a small hatch – and it weighs next to nothing. Try pushing a galvanised metal tank up into a loft and you'll never want to do it again! The plastic tanks are easy to connect, and of course they won't rust, corrode, or burst. But just a word of warning. Don't heave yourself up into the loft by means of a pipe connected to a plastic tank. You may end up being soaked.

Your tank should have a cover on it to keep out dirt and other undesirable objects. And the tank needs lagging, too, if it is in the loft. Either build a simple box around the tank (if square) or use expanded polystyrene sheet or glass-fibre blanket. Cover the lid too, leaving a hole for water from the expansion pipe to go through. An ordinary plastic funnel is a good idea for directing water into the tank.

Always leave the bottom of the tank unlagged so a little warmth reaches it from the rooms below. And be sure to lag pipes connected to the tank. For extra protection, you could fit a tank immersion heater which gets warm enough just to keep the chill off the water during a really cold spell. Don't forget that it has to be switched on before you get a really severe freeze.

PLUMBING TIPS

First, let's expose a common fallacy. If an emergency such as a burst water storage tank should occur, the right thing to do is to open all taps and drain the system after tying up the ball valve in the loft. Some folk say that this means the hot tank in the airing cupboard is drained too – with danger of a boiler explosion. In fact, you cannot drain the hot water cylinder by means of the hot taps because the feed to the taps is taken from the *top* of the tank, and pressure to push the water comes from the cold water storage tank – which is the one being drained.

So all is well, even if the boiler fire is left in, as long as you don't roar it up. Similarly the boiler cannot be emptied this way. To drain boiler and cylinder you have to drain off at the drain cock, usually situated at the base of the boiler itself. And you won't get an explosion because the vent pipe is designed to release any build-up in pressure.

Secondly, how can one get rid of the horrible trickling noise in the cold water storage tank? You can usually eliminate it by fitting a silencer tube to the ball valve. If you feel just below the actual hinge pin you should find a threaded hole, and into this you screw the plastic silencer tube – available cheaply from any plumbers' merchants. By the way, you are supposed to drill a small hole near the top of the tube, if there isn't one already. This will prevent what is called back-siphoning should the mains water supply fail. Air entering through the hole breaks the siphon.

Folk often ask how they can stop the horrible shhhhh noise which can be heard intermittently in the plumbing system as the tank refills. This is usually caused by water ripples on the surface bobbing the ball up and down, which in turn opens and closes the valve. You can never completely lose the noise – especially in modern copper plumbing – but you can often reduce it in one of two ways. First, by bending the ball valve arm in a horizontal plane (so the ball is no lower or higher in the water, but merely off-set slightly). Second, by tying to the ball arm a plastic colander so that the colander is suspended beneath the water. This has a damping effect on the ball float, again reducing the noise. It will also help eliminate the noise we call water hammer.

If you have any leaky pipe threads and the nuts won't tighten any more, don't mess about with red lead and frayed string. Ask for some ptfe tape. You bind the thread with this then tighten your nut over it and, presto, you have a perfect mess-free joint.

CHAPTER NINE
Electrics

FOR RED, READ BROWN
This is the age of conformity, and millions of pounds are being spent to make us as much like all other Europeans as possible. Metric money we have taken in our stride. Metric measurements are causing a certain amount of confusion. And one other change made some time ago is still causing confusion. It is the change of colour coding in certain electrical wiring.

Three-core flex, such as is fixed to electric irons, washing machines and power tools, as from July 1, 1970, has the new colours brown (live), blue (neutral), and green/yellow stripes (earth). All new appliances sold since that time must have been fitted with the new colour flex but, of course, existing appliances bearing the old colours (red, live; black, neutral; green, earth) are still O.K.

The brown wire is for live, and always goes to the live terminal of a plug. The blue wire is for neutral and must go to the neutral terminal. The green/yellow striped wire is for earth and must go to the earth terminal.

At the time of writing, the new code is not mandatory for two-core flex. But most cable makers are producing two-core flexes with brown and blue cores to avoid confusion.

This new colour coding does *not*, however, apply to wiring cable used for heating and lighting circuits. It applies only to flexibles. So when you extend the house wiring you will still find the old colours.

Although a lot has been said about colour codings, this isn't all that has happened to your wiring. We have also lost (since early 1970) our old system of classifying cables and flexes. As you probably know, you would order, say, three yards of 7/.029, which meant the cable had seven separate wires, each 0.029

BEGINNER'S GUIDE TO DO-IT-YOURSELF

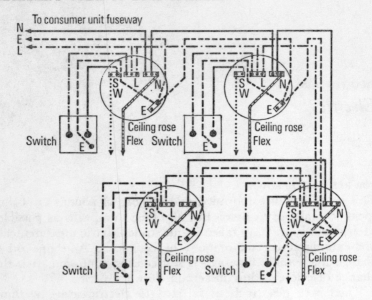

Wiring – loop-in method

Key to wiring colours
—·—·— Red
———— Black
— — — Green
—··—··— Yellow
▬▬▬▬ Blue
········ Brown

in. in diameter. That is all swept away, and now a system using a metric cross-sectional area is in force.

So, for house wiring, a lighting circuit previously wired in 3/.029 you get 1.0 mm^2 (that is one wire of one square millimetre cross-sectional area). For your ring circuit, you now use 2.5 mm^2 and for a 30-amp cooker circuit 4.0 mm^2.

A similar system has been introduced for flexibles, so instead of seeing 23/.0076 you will see the flex is referred to as 24/.20 which means 24 wires, each 0.20 mm diameter. And you will find new 10-amp, 15-amp and 20-amp flexible cords have been introduced.

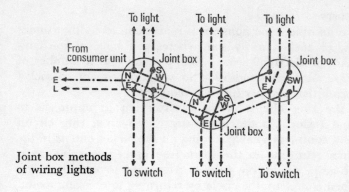

Joint box methods of wiring lights

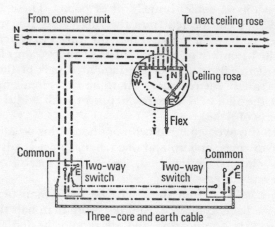

A two-way switching circuit

Other changes have been made, but the only other worth mentioning here is fuse ratings. For an old 15-amp system the fuse wires stay the same, but with a 13-amp system where cartridge fuses are used, there are now only two sizes of fuse – 3-amp and 13-amp. And don't let anyone tell you different! The 3-amp fuse is coloured blue and will take appliances up to 720 watts. The 13-amp fuse is brown, and this will take appliances between 720 and 3,120 watts.

It is not all that complicated really, but if you do get into deep water, it is best to go to a good electrical shop and ask them for advice. This may not necessarily be your local Electricity Board showroom, many of which seem to be electricity supermarkets now.

RING CIRCUITS

If yours is an older-type house, it is more than likely that under the stairs, or tucked away somewhere, you have a fine conglomeration of electrical wiring disappearing into a number of fuses boxes. And every addition to your assortment of socket outlets meant that another fuse was required.

Well, the ring circuit offers a revolution in approach to wiring and fusing. As the name suggests, with a ring circuit you have a continuous cable feeding all the socket outlets in the house, then returning to the main fuse unit. The cable starts at the 30-amp, single-pole fuse, is connected to various socket outlets, then completes the circle by returning to the same point. In addition, cables branch off at points. These are called spurs, and they can be fed from the ring cable. But there are certain rules to bear in mind. First, the ring circuit can feed an unlimited number of socket outlets of the 13-amp fused plug type, but if the floor area of the inhabited part of the house exceeds 100 square metres, more than one ring circuit must be installed – at the rate of one extra circuit for each additional 100 square metres of floor area.

In the average three-bedroom house this usually only amounts to two rings, one up and one down. But it is advised that if two ring circuits are involved, that the number of outlets is shared as evenly as possible.

Secondly, a spur must feed no more than two socket outlets or one fixed appliance. And not more than half the total number of sockets on the ring and spurs may be fed from spurs. For example, if you have 18 socket outlets in all planned for your ring system, no more than nine of these may be fed from spurs. When a fixed appliance is installed, a fused spur unit is used instead of the normal socket outlet and plug. These are available with or without a switch, and there is a type with a small pilot light – very useful if a water heater is installed.

As mentioned earlier, 13-amp 3-pin plugs are used, of the fused variety, with a choice of 3- and 13-amp fuses. The fused plugs protect the various applicances, and the whole circuit is protected by a 30-amp fuse which will blow only if an attempt is made to overload the circuit. As you will by now appreciate, the whole system is far easier and neater than the old methods of wiring; and installing such a system is well within the capabilities of a careful handyman. Many thousands of installations

ELECTRICS

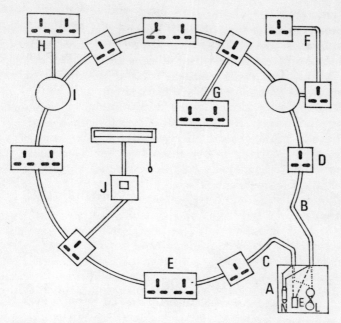

A typical ring circuit. A. Main switch. B. & C. Circuit cable. D. Single socket outlet. E. Double socket outlet. F. Spur. G. & H. Double spurs. I. Junction box. J. Switched connection unit.

have been made by now, and we have yet to hear of complaint from the local Electricity Boards.

The necessary items can be obtained from any good electrical shop. The cable used is 2.5 mm² twin core plus earth. The same cable is used for the spurs. Finally, it is the job of an Electricity Board official to connect your new circuit to your meter. Don't try to do *that* yourself!

FUSES

When the man of the house is away from home, a fuse decides to blow! So, ladies, how do you mend a fuse? A fuse is a deliberate weak link in an electrical circuit. If something goes wrong, the fuse wire melts, leaving the rest of the system undamaged and safe. Why does a fuse go? There are three main reasons.

First, the fuse wire may just have eroded with age, and for no other reason. Second, the path of the electrical current may have been short-circuited, in which case there will be a bang, and the wire will disappear. Third, the circuit may have been overloaded. Too many appliances will cause the fuse wire to overheat. No bang; it will just melt away.

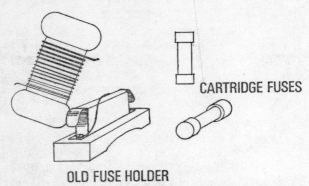

Fuse wire, a rewirable fuse holder, and cartridge fuses

If yours is an older property, you will have a collection of fuse boxes and switches. And if you are sensible, there will be a plan hanging up nearby showing just which box controls what. This will save all the time otherwise needed to pull out every fuse and examine it, if you've no idea which is which.

You will find the fuse carrier pulls out – but not before the switch is off, remember! Some fuse boxes can't be opened until the switch is off, and this is a very sensible idea.

Examine the thin wire and ensure that it is intact. If it is, push the carrier back and check the next. If not, the wire must be replaced with equivalent fuse wire; 5-amp for lighting and 10-amp and 15-amp for power. Thread a length of wire, and secure it behind the retaining screws. Replace the fuse carrier and switch on.

If there is another bang, something is shorting. It may be your iron; a table lamp; a faulty electric fire – or whatever you have recently plugged in. Pull out suspect appliances and try again.

If the fuse melted again, you must cut the load. You may have too many fires on at once.

ELECTRICS

If yours is a modern house, you will more likely than not have a 13-amp system with square pin plugs and in-built fuses. And you may have a consumer unit instead of a mass of fuse boxes. Under the Institution of Electrical Engineers regulations only two fuse sizes are required; 3-amp and 13-amp – but you may well still find some 2-amp and 10-amp ones in use. The 3-amp is intended for portable lamps, televisions, radios and other small appliances. The 13-amp will do the rest, up to and including 3 kW.

The beauty of this system is that any fault is usually localised. If you have a faulty standard lamp – say the flex has become disconnected – the fuse will blow in the fused plug connected to it. Open up the plug, after withdrawing it from the socket, and replace the fuse. Look for the fault, and if you are unable to correct it, leave the appliance until the man of the house gets in.

Now a couple of tips. If the light does go out, don't be too hasty in your fuse replacing. The bulb may have burned out! Try another bulb first. Also try other lights in the house. If all are out, just have a peep across the road. You may have a power cut which no amount of fuse changing will cure! If there is a cut, your neighbours will be in the dark too.

Finally, be prepared. You should have a card of new fuse wire or spare cartridge fuses – or both; an insulated electrician's screwdriver and a torch that works, stood neatly near those fuse boxes. And, of course, the plan of the system, mentioned earlier, hanging nearby. With these items at hand, plus a little plain commonsense and care, you won't be kept in the dark for long.

WIRE THAT PLUG!

Every time you buy a new electrical gadget, you have to fit a plug to the flex. It is surprising, therefore, that so many folk do it wrong. Whatever the system – old 5- and 15-amp round-pin sockets or modern 13-amp square types – the principle is the same.

Looking at a three-pin *socket*, with the big earth hole at the top, the connections are: top, earth; bottom left, neutral; bottom right, live. From this you can see which terminals are which inside the *plug*, when the cover is removed. If you have bought a new appliance and are not just fitting a plug to an old one, remember that the core colours of the flex will be green/yellow stripes for earth; brown for live; and blue for neutral.

If there are only two wires in the flex, it means that the appliance is double insulated — no part of the device that can be touched is electrically connected to the motor or other electrical part. So no earth wire is needed. It just means connecting the blue wire to the neutral pin and the brown wire to the live pin.

When preparing a flex for connection to a plug, first remove about $1\frac{1}{2}$ in. of the protective sheath, being careful not to damage the insulation around the conductors. Then, holding the flex so that the end of the sheath is just over the flex clamp or anchor, cut each conductor so that it is about $\frac{1}{4}$ in. longer than necessary to reach its terminal (for wind-around terminals, allow $\frac{1}{2}$ in.).

Strip about $\frac{3}{8}$ in. of insulation from the ends of the conductors, twist the wires and, if the flex is a thin one, double the conductor back on itself to give the terminal screw something solid to pinch (for wind-arounds, twist and wrap the free end of bare wire clockwise around the terminal post, so that the tightening of the nut will tend to give it a firmer grip, rather than unwind it).

Insert the conductor in the hole and tighten the clamp screw. Neatly position the wires inside the plug so they do not get pinched, fix the sheath in the anchor device — most important — and replace fuse and cover.

Index

Adhesives, 60
Aerosols, 57
Alarms, burglar, 68
Animal glues, 60
Anti-condensation paint, 117
Asphalt, cold, for paths, 27

Ball valves, 138, 144
Bending hardboard, 48
Boiler ventilation, 132
Brick bonds, 30
Brickwork, painting, 33
Brickwork, porous, 118
Burglar alarms, 68

Carpet, stair, 95
Casein glue, 61
Cavity insulation, 127
Ceiling repairs, 72
Central heating, 136
Ceramic wall tiles, 70
Chipboard, veneered, 50
Cladding walls, 35
Cleaning old furniture, 78
Cold water storage tank, 145
Colour codes, for wiring, 149
Condensation, 88, 116
Condensation in flues, 101
Contact adhesive, 50, 61
Copper pipework, 139
Cove cornice, 74
Curtain rails, 96
Cutting chipboard, 51
Cutting glass, 55
Cutting plastic laminates, 48

Damp-proof course, 120
Damp, rising, 88, 120
Damp, structural, 118
Decorated hardboard, 47
Decorating, 106
Descaling hot water systems, 139
Designs for chipboard furniture, 51
Distemper, 109
Dividing a room, 103
Door locks, 65
Doors, ready made, 54
Double glazing, 126
Dowelling jig, 52
Dowels, 81
Draughts, 129
Dry rot, 83
Dry rot, in floors, 120

Edging strip for chipboard, 52
Electrics, 149
Epoxy resin adhesives, 60
Expanded polystyrene ceiling tiles, 109
Extractor fans, 117, 132

Fans, extractor, 132
Fence repairs, 10
Fences in kits, 10
Fences – various types, 9
Filter units, for kitchens, 133
Fireplace, blocking off, 102
Fire ventilators, 132
Fixing curtain rails, 97
Flashings, damaged, 118

INDEX

Floorboard gaps, curing, 91
Floorboards, lifting, 90
Floorcoverings, hardboard, 47, 90
Floor levelling, 84
Floor panels, 87
Floor sanding machine, 91
Floors, damp, 120
Floors, solid, 88
Floors, timber, 89
Floor tiles, 84
Flue linings, 101
Flue troubles, 101
Flue ventilation, 103
Freeze-up, 133
Fungicidal plugs, 122
Fuses, 151, 153

Gaps between floorboards, 91
Gaps, various, 91
Gates, repairs to, 13
Glass and glazing, 54
Glues, 60
Gutter guards, 37
Gutters and downpipes, damaged, 118
Gutters, fitting new, 35

Hammer drill, 40
Hardboard, 46
Hardboard, as floor coverings, 47, 90
Hardboard, bending, 48
Hardboard, conditioning, 90
Hardwood floor, reconditioning, 91
Hatchway, making, 99
Heating in workshop, 20
Hire of tools, 63
Hot water systems, descaling, 139

Insulation of cold water tank, 146

Jointing chipboard, 51
Jointing methods, 81

Kitchen ventilation, 132
Knock-down fittings, 82

Ladder brackets, 44
Ladder safety, 42

Laminated plastic, 48
Leaks, central heating, 136
Lintels, fixing to, 97
Lock lubrication, 57
Locks, 65
Lofts, 104
Longhorn beetle, 83
Lubrication, 56
Lubrication, curtain rails, 98

Masonry, fixing to, 39
Metal protection, 56
Metric wiring, 149
Modernising stairways, 93

Noise, 123

Oils, 56
Old furniture, cleaning, 78

Pad brushes, 57
Painting brickwork, 33
Painting tips, 32, 106
Painting with aerosols and pad brushes, 57
Painting woodwork, 110
Paint removing, 78
Paint stripping, 109
Parquet flooring, 87
Paths, concrete, 21
Paths, repairs, 25
Paving, precast, 24
Paving slabs, making, 23
Pegboard, 46
Picture rail removal, 107
Pipe joints, 140
Plasterboard fixing, 45
Plaster cracks, 92
Plaster repairs, 72
Plastic cold water tanks, 146
Plastic gutters, 35
Plastic joints, 81
Plastic laminates, 48
Plastics in plumbing, 141
Plugging walls, 98
Plug wiring, 155
Plumbing, freeze-ups, 129, 133
Plumbing, plastics in, 141
Plumbing system, 137

INDEX

Plumbing tips, 147
Pointing, renewing, 37
Pointing, types, 37
Polystyrene ceiling tiles, 109
Polystyrene wall tiles, 70
Preparation, for decorating, 108
Protection from intruders, 64
PVA adhesives, 60

Quarry tiles, 84, 88

Radiator leaks, 137
Radiator shelves, 80
Ring circuits, 152
Rising damp, 88, 120
Room dividing, 103
Room in the loft, 104
Rough textured walls, 114
Rubber base glue, 61
Rust protection, 56

Sacrificial anode, 146
Safety on a ladder, 42
Sanding machine, for floors, 91
Scaffold kit, 44
Screeding compounds, 84, 88
Security, 64
Shelving, 80
Silencer, cold water tank, 138, 147
Sink units, ready made, 54
Solid floors, 88
Spurs for fence posts, 11
Squeaks, in stairs, 93
Stair carpets, 95
Staircase, ready made, 54
Stair repairs, 92
Standard joinery, 53
Steam stripper, 63, 74
Stripping block, 110

Tack rag, 110
Taps and washers, 142
Tap washer renewal, 137, 142
Tarmac, cold, for paths, 27

Tiles, floor, 84
Tiles, roof, damaged, 118
Tiles, wall, 70
Timber floors, 89
Timber, preservative treatments, 15
Timber, troubles, 82
Tool hire, 63
Tools, 62
Tower scaffold, 44

Varnish removing, 78
Veneered chipboard, 50
Ventilation of flue, 103
Ventilators, for fires, 132

Wall cladding, 35
Wallcoverings, removal, 109
Wall insulation, 127
Wallpaper hanging, 110
Wallpaper troubles, 112
Walls, fixings to, 39, 98
Walls, garden, building, 28
Walls, porous, 118
Wall tiles, 70
Washable wallcoverings, removal, 109
Water tank in the loft, 145
Water tank, silencer, 138, 147
Weatherproofing walls, 34
Whitewood, finishing, 76
Window frame gaps, 92, 119
Window locks, 67
Windows, double glazing, 126
Windows, ready made, 54
Wiring a plug, 155
Wiring colours, new, 149
Wiring lights, 150
Wiring, two-way circuit, 151
Wood block flooring, 87
Wood lubrication, 57
Woodworm, 82
Workshop, heating, 20
Workshop, insulation, 19
Workshop, weatherproofing, 18